RECLAIMING
Your Addicted Brain

A Recovery GPS: How to find your path to
Recovery and not get lost along the way

IRWIN MORSE AND **ROGER STARK**

Blessing one day at a time!

Roger & Irwin

Silver Star Publishing

Silver Star Publishing
3942 Krause Ct.
Washougal, WA 98671

Printing in the United States of America
ISBN: 978-0-692-69631-6

DEDICATION

This book is dedicated to the addict who still suffers —
there is no deeper abyss for the human soul.

And, To Sues in our lives: Thanks for waiting.

CONTENTS

INTRODUCTION

Addiction recovery can be an elusive beast. Recovery from the sexual addictions is an elusive beast that enjoys taking steroids. It manifests as newbies struggle in their recovery, attending meetings, meeting with a sponsor, maybe even visiting with a therapist, but merely marching in place, not really being "in" or moving forward in recovery at all.

The problem? The Monkey Brain. The moniker that describes the collection of thinking errors, denials, rationalizations, justifications, character defects, and behaviors that allow perfectly good people to transition their reality to a place that allows and justifies sexual acting out. Think of this book as "prep school" for recovery, Get these principles in place and your recovery will not mark time, but take off like a rocket.

Two voices will appear throughout the document:

The "**Narrator**" tells the story in this font.

"George" *presents his recovery from sexual addiction story in this font. His comments and views will appear throughout the narrative and will always appear with his name at the beginning of the section.*

Chapter 1

Defining the Monkey Brain
Investigating the Problem

Inexplicable logic is normal fare in addict land. Friends and family are baffled by the behaviors, antics, and thinking of the addicted one. Their patience, tolerance, and love are depleted quickly. Eventually their empathy and compassion exhausted, they say the inevitable, "He will just have to hit bottom," as they shake their heads and walk away.

The tool of self-destruction so effectively wielded by the addict is his own mind. The addict takes a perfectly good brain and, by relying on thinking errors, rationalization, justification, and every form of denial known to man, creates what might rightly be called the "Monkey Brain" of addiction. Perfect for conducting the work of addiction, it relentlessly delivers the self-inflicted wounds that are the addict's stock in trade that, unchecked, lead to his/her demise.

No disrespect to our distant cousins, the monkey, intended. There is a reason they have Monkey Brains—they are monkeys after all. Monkey Brains in humans is a different matter. This defective mind is created by convolutions in thinking and life processing. The reality for the addicted brain is, "Your best thinking got you here, and your current best thinking will not get your out!"

Our use of the term "Monkey Brain" is based on the Buddhist term "Mind Monkey," *xinyuan* in Chinese, meaning "unsettled; restless; capricious; whimsical; fanciful; inconstant; confused; indecisive; uncontrollable." (https://en.wikipedia.org/wiki/Mind_monkey)

We use Monkey Brain to mean the combination of faulty thinking, lack of good judgment, flawed boundaries, and loss of contact with one's personal truth. It means the sufferer is disconnected from reality. The addict creates a reality that only they understand, with rules that make sense only to them. To put it another way, the Monkey Brain is convinced up is down, down is up, left is right, and right is left.

With a Monkey Brain in place, addicts don't think like normal folks. That is part of the bafflement for friends and family members; they are not privy to the addict's reality. It makes no sense to them; it is just not the world they are living in.

When friends say, "You're going to lose your job," a fact obvious to all except the addict, the addict's Monkey Brain is not penetrated by the truth of it. Too many justifications and rationalizations protect the addict's reasoning from believing or embracing any such talk.

The Monkey Brain starts puking out justifications and defenses:

"Yeah, I probably drink a little too much. But heavens, I'm not a heroin addict for crying out loud."

"Oh things got messy a while back, but I have really cut down, I know my limits now."

"I'll only drink on the weekends" or "I'll give up the hard stuff and stick to beer."

"I've battled this for 40 years and haven't won. No need to think I can now."

"It's those guys I work with. They always drag me along, and they make fun of me if I don't keep up with them."

"Maybe I do drink too much, but hell, it's my life and I will live it how I want."

These are Monkey Brain deductions. All have one result: they make recovery impossible and keep the addiction in the addict's life.

These Are Self-Inflicted Wounds

If autopsies were conducted on addicts, the most prevalent contributing cause listed would be: "Death by addiction due to self-inflicted wounds." These self-inflicted wounds occur when the Monkey Brain is running the show. One addict starts, "I got all up in my head," when explaining his acting out and the latest relapse damage report. What addict doesn't relish a world-class pity party on his way to enjoying his addiction? These are self-inflicted wounds.

Many deal with issues not of their own making like unrequested trauma and genetic or cultural issues not of their choosing. These maladies require their own special therapeutic solutions, but the self-inflicted wounds fall within personal accountability and there are options. There are skills that can mitigate these.

Recovery might even be described as the process of learning or gaining the skills to stop the carnage. Addicts have the power to stop shooting themselves in the foot … or head, as the case may be.

A good place to start is by turning off the Monkey Brain and putting it into storage. Skills like self-awareness, the quieting of self, accountability, and living in this particular moment help accomplish that. The hopeful truth of Recovery is that "with repeated and direct attention towards a desired change we all have the ability to rewire our brains." (Alta Mira Recovery)

Quite interestingly, in the depths of addiction, addicts are absolutely convinced self-inflicted wounds are administered by the hands of others. "People don't listen to me; I'm always getting screwed over." In short order the addict is offended; in the fertile soils of the Monkey Brain, gargantuan resentments are grown (perennials that never stop blooming). Nothing remotely close to personal accountability ever enters the addict's garden or penetrates the Monkey Brain.

The Monkey Brain spawns the wounds. Insecurity, fear, jealousy, anger, self-righteousness, and their many close cousins father the daggers that cut one's emotional flesh. Their toxic, infectious nature chokes out serenity, integrity, duty, honor, compassion, humility, and healing and leaves festering wounds with condemnation to repeated addictive behaviors.

And guess whose fingerprints are all over the daggers?

Monkey Brain in Action — just how crazy is crazy?

George was married for 35 years and his addiction was having affairs with women outside his marriage. Over the years these affairs ranged from one-night stands to an affair that lasted more than five years. He will describe where his Monkey Brain thinking took him.

George: *At my girlfriend's suggestion, I went to a week-long intensive therapy program to treat alcoholism (which is what we both thought I had), but the intake group determined my real problem was sex addiction and put me in that group. The week was very helpful, and I learned a lot about the Pia Melody model, trauma, the inner child, the addict cycle, and treatment options. My post-program sobriety action plan included going to AA and SAA meetings, to start working with a CSAT therapist, and to not drink or have any contact with my old affair partners.*

I did all of these things, some more avidly than others. I found weekly AA and SAA meetings and a therapist recommended by the program I had attended. Not drinking never seemed to be the problem. I figured that I had already been sober for a few weeks so why not see if I could continue longer.

However, early in the process I started suffering from withdrawal from my lack of contact with my affair partner. The first week or so was fine, but shortly after that I started feeling the loss of not having this person in my life any longer. The thought of her never being part of my life again was just too painful. After all, she did nothing wrong and was my confidante who knew more about me than anyone else.

At the same time I was starting to feel better and wanted to share that progress with her and jump forward to make Step 9 amends, despite the fact that I had not yet completed Step 1.

About this time I was returning from an overseas flight through LA and had a four-hour layover. While in the waiting lounge I struck up a conversation with a fellow passenger who lived in the same city as my affair partner. This fellow thought he knew her and promised to send my regards.

This is when my Monkey Brain came out with a series of great ideas. First, why rely

on this complete stranger to handle such an important communication? He was probably not going to do anything anyway. Why not eliminate the risk and do this myself?

Now this presented a dilemma since my counselor asked every week if I had
been in contact with my affair partner. To resolve this issue, my Monkey Brain
came up with this brilliant solution: I would create a fake person, with an email
account, name, address, and personal history and use that person to contact
her. She would communicate with this third person and he would forward the
communication to me. Of course the two of us were the same person. But if
questioned, I could easily show the email trail to prove there was someone in
the middle. Smart!!!

This way I could "honestly" answer the question, "Have you been in contact
with your paramour?" by saying, "No I haven't contacted her, but I am in touch
with someone who knows her." What could be wrong with that?

The communications started and the process went very well, just as I had
hoped. It continued for several weeks. However, I was not content with this
level of communication. I desperately wanted to see her again. So to this end I
manipulated the situation by telling this third party that I was going to be in a
particular city for a conference and wouldn't it be great if she surprised me by
showing up at the hotel bar. The plan worked great. She showed up and we met.
I convinced myself there was nothing bad going on because we just talked and
stayed in separate rooms and never had sex.

Several weeks afterwards, I was in my therapist's office and she asked, "Have
you been in contact with your old girlfriend?"

I said, "You know, the funniest thing happened. I ran into her at a conference
I attended recently; she just happened to be there."

The therapist sensed something rotten in Denmark and started probing for
details of how this happened. As a result, all of the details started to unravel
and I told the whole story of what I had done.

The therapist looked at me in a stony silence and said, "George, you are really
screwed up and need serious help. An hour once a week isn't going to make a
dent in your issues." I wound up going into a three-week intensive program, not
really understanding what she was so excited about.

An interesting sideline comment and a testament to how conniving addicts *can be. When I did finally make amends to my girlfriend and told her what I had done she did not believe me. She thought this other person actually existed. No amount of explanation could convince her otherwise.*

And Now, Some Therapizing

From the Clinic: Let's look at George's narrative again.

George: *At my girlfriend's suggestion, I went to a week-long intensive therapy program to treat alcoholism (which is what we both thought I had), but the intake group determined my real problem was sex addiction and put me in that group.*

From the Clinic: Addict George was without awareness of his true situation. His Monkey Brain thinking would not allow him that kind of clarity. It is hard to find solutions when you don't even know what the problems are. This is the lot of those new to recovery. The Monkey Brain has not been vanquished and its deductions continue to get in the way.

George: *I did all of these things, some more avidly than others. I found weekly AA and SAA meetings and a therapist recommended by the program I had attended. Not drinking never seemed to be the problem. I figured that I had already been sober for a few weeks so why not see if I could continue longer.*

From the Clinic: At this point, George has the appearance of beginning recovery, but as his story unfolds you will see that George was not invested in the process. The appearance of recovery does not lead to recovery. And periods of sobriety don't necessarily mean recovery either. Many invest years in meetings, therapists, and sponsors and never have much recovery at all. A Monkey Brain will do that to you. At some point we must be "all in," and this work of recovery must penetrate to our very souls.

George: *However, early in the process I started suffering from withdrawal from my lack of contact with my affair partner. The first week or so was fine, but shortly* *after that I started feeling the loss of not having this person in my life any longer. The thought of her never being part of my life again was just too painful. After all, she did nothing wrong and was my confidante who knew more about me than anyone else.*

From the Clinic: Ah yes, withdrawal. That nasty thing that happens when we cannot use our drug of choice anymore. It is also an "on" switch for our Monkey Brain to find acting-out solutions. His Monkey Brain produces a couple of real gems for George: "The thought of her never being part of my life again was just too painful." A victim stance, eliciting falsely created sympathy, this smacks of me, me, me, me, me. (Please refer to the first line of George's story, the part about MARRIED for 35 years.) A sponsor would suggest George's first and only obligation should be to his spouse and stopping the causes of her pain.

Then come the classic double-thinking errors, "After all she did nothing wrong," and "[she] was my confidante who knew more about me than anyone else." Both are Monkey Brain masterpieces. Pleading for fairness, "she did nothing wrong," "she was my confidante," but the fairness meter George is using is skewed over to "I want what I want, when I want it" mode. It ignores the damage he is doing to his spouse and ignores the fact he is selfishly using his girlfriend, offering her little in return. For George in Monkey Brain mode, all his logic sounds soooo true and convincing.

George: *At the same time I was starting to feel better and wanted to share that progress with her and jump forward to make Step 9 amends, despite the fact that I had not yet completed Step 1.*

From the Clinic: Here is a common rookie mistake. Getting ahead of ourselves. They are called steps and are in an order for a reason. They are a path we follow. The order is important. The rookie, with Monkey Brain fully engaged, plows right into Step 9 work with exuberance and pride born of self-righteous arrogance. "See, I am working my program," he justifies. Well, not really, the program starts with step 1, "sharing progress" with his victim was just a guise for further contact.

George: *About this time I was returning from an overseas flight through LA and had a four-hour layover. While in the waiting lounge I struck up a conversation with a fellow passenger who lived in the same city as my affair partner. This fellow thought he knew her and promised to send my regards.*

This is when my Monkey Brain came out with a series of great ideas. First, why rely on this complete stranger to handle such an important communication. He was probably not going to do anything anyway. Why not eliminate the risk and do this myself?

From the Clinic: George's Monkey Brain is fully engaged now, and off to the races. With the justification fully in place (I need to make my amends to her!), it is only a matter of figuring out a few details, which, for the Monkey Brain is really no challenge at all.

George: *Now this presented a dilemma since my counselor asked every week if I had been in contact with my affair partner. To resolve this issue, my Monkey Brain came up with this brilliant solution: I would create a fake person, with an email account, name, address, and personal history and use that person to contact her. She would communicate with this third person and he would forward the communication to me. Of course the two of us were the same person. But if questioned, I could easily show the email trail to prove there was someone in the middle. Smart!!!*

This way I could "honestly" answer the question, "Have you been in contact with your paramour?" by saying. "No I haven't contacted her, but I am in touch with someone who knows her." What could be wrong with that?

From the Clinic: What could possibly be wrong with that? In Monkey Brain land this is perfectly logical, even noble. But in the real world where integrity, honesty, marriage vows and such matter, it does not pass the smell test.

George: *The communications started and the process went very well, just as I had hoped. It continued for several weeks. However, I was not content with* *this level of communication. I desperately wanted to see her again. So to this end I manipulated the situation by telling this third party that I was going to be in a particular city for a conference and wouldn't it be great if she surprised me by showing up at the hotel bar. The plan worked great. She showed up and we met. I convinced myself there was nothing bad going on because we just talked and stayed in separate rooms and never had sex.*

From the Clinic: "Just talked and never had sex." (justification/rationalization) Too little too late, for something that never should have happened. Smart people are especially susceptible to Monkey Brain Syndrome. Their minds are capable of high intellectual achievement and when turned lose with Monkey Brain standards, the rationalizations and justifications are especially convincing. They contain just enough truth, often emote enough false sympathy and compassion, that the addict can ignore the totally erroneous foundations.

George: *Several weeks afterwards, I was in my therapist's office and she asked, "Have you been in contact with your old girlfriend?"*

I said, "You know, the funniest thing happened. I ran into her at a conference I attended recently; she just happened to be there."

The therapist sensed something rotten in Denmark and started probing for details of how this happened. As a result, all of the details started to unravel and I told the whole story of what I had done.

From the Clinic: The therapist recognized Monkey Brain activity and called George on his thinking errors. This kind of accountability is indispensable for any newcomer wanting to navigate to recovery. As long as the Monkey Brain is on and working, the addict will be in addict mode. Attending meetings and working with sponsors and a therapist can bring the power of accountability, putting honesty and integrity back into the addict's life.

Fundamental accountability, of course, lies with the addict. Learning to recognize when his Monkey Brain is "on" and spewing is critical. Acting out will not end until the addict turns the Monkey Brain to "off" and no longer accepts its nonsense rationalizations and justifications.

George: *The therapist looked at me in a stony silence and said, "George, you are really screwed up and need serious help. An hour once a week isn't going to make a dent in your issues." I wound up going into a three-week intensive program, not really understanding what she was so excited about.*

An interesting sideline comment and a testament to how conniving addicts can be. When I did finally make amends to my girlfriend and told her what I had done she did not believe me. She thought this other person actually existed.

From the Clinic: What a testimony to the power of Monkey Brain work, its ability to convince, and the degree of dysfunction of our addictive relationships. Our victims cannot see reality themselves. If they could they would be of no interest to us.

Understanding More About the Monkey Brain

George: *The foundations for the monkey brain are established early in life. Likely between the time a child's conscious mind is taking form and the first time the word "no" is heard in response to a demand. Up to that point the child's paradigm is straightforward: ask for what you want and get it. If the child wants food, to be picked up, all he/she need do is cry and the needs are met. They are not subject to any reasonableness test and require no justification or explanation.*

About the time of the first "no" the need satisfaction paradigm is changed. Now there are constraints on getting wants and needs met. Need satisfaction comes with other parameters: they are judged as being reasonable, timely, legitimate (or not). When the need is expressed by the child and not met, he/she wonders what has changed. Why are they being denied what they used to get without question or justification?

Often cited as the "terrible twos," this is a normal phase of development. However, our theory is that this is where the addict mind/Monkey Brain takes root. To help rationalize and understand this new paradigm the child taps into the components of the Monkey Brain: anger, entitlement, rage, and revenge. Healthy children move in and out of these emotions quickly. Those prone to addiction tend to live in these emotions for longer periods, assessing everything in the context "why me?" and calling upon these emotional responses to manipulate the situation to get their needs met.

Addicts have one thing in common, be they sex addicts, alcoholics, gamblers, whatever: they will do almost anything—no matter how insane—to get their needs met. It does not matter how safe or unsafe, rational or irrational. When the addict brain is in charge the mantra is "damn the torpedoes, full speed ahead."

One addict axiom is, "I want what I want and I want it now." When those wants are not satisfied in the Monkey Brain the pressure builds until the addict acts out and gets what he/she wants. The tolerance for "need denial" determines the level and frequency of acting out.

As such, the Monkey Brain's goal is to medicate, nothing else. It is a pleasure center-driven brain, hedonistic, self-absorbed, and not subject to constraints. Nothing is off limits, is too wild or crazy. Its sole objective is to make the person feel better, to remove the anger, address the entitlement, quash the rage, and satisfy the need for revenge.

Half-Truths

The MB (Monkey Brain) creates what the recovery world recognizes as stinkin' thinkin', the great sustainer of addictive behaviors. It is the creator of rationalization, justification and all their cousins. It generates the logic that separates one from reality and allows the making of really bad decisions and the becoming of really good addicts.

George: My Monkey Brain tries to convince me something is true, i.e., reality, or a good idea; that is really crazy. I use the word "reality" purposefully as when I am under the control of my Monkey Brain I am convinced I am in reality.

I remember a video showing a man in lab apparel, sitting in front of a lab desk and talking to the camera about perception. He was discussing what your mind accepts as reality based on the input it receives, particularly from the eyes.

As the monologue progresses, the camera begins to rotate. What you realize as it finishes its rotation is that the man is actually sitting on the ceiling. He is upside down but the room was made to make it look like he was right side up, thereby demonstrating how easy it is for the mind to be tricked.

I used the following example of this in my work when talking about control systems and what we see and what we take for granted.

Every night at 5:10 p.m. Chuck rolls a wheelbarrow full of sand up to the security gate before exiting the plant. Dutifully the guard sifts through the sand looking for anything that Chuck might have hidden there to try to steal—tools or copper wire for example. After satisfying himself that there is nothing there, the guard waves him through. This goes on every day for a month.

After a month of this, the guard's curiosity can no longer be contained. He asks, "Chuck, what are you doing with all that sand?"

Chuck looks at him and says, "Nothing, I'm stealing wheelbarrows."

Your addict utilizes your Monkey Brain to manipulate you into seeing things it wants you to see and not what is really there. Often, this convinces you that a bad behavior is actually good or comes with no risk. It uses expressions like:

"I was just wondering ..."

"This is the last time I'll ..."

"Everyone else is doing it ..."

"No one will ever know ..."

"Just this once ..."

"I deserve this ..."

"I can handle this alone ..."

"I don't care ..."

It hides behind outright lies and half-truths, and justifies certain behaviors as cultural norms even though these thoughts are dangerous and detrimental.

I recall one time a therapist said, "Many people think it is normal to drink too much and get behind the wheel of a car, but that doesn't make it right or a good idea."

Some Background

The Monkey Brain is an agent for the Emotional Management System (EMS). It is in charge of filling orders. MB "won the contract," so when an urge is created by the EMS, the Monkey Brain is mandated with finding a way to make it happen.

The Emotional Management System is charged with finding solutions to emotional needs. The EMS is always looking for ways to comfort difficult feelings. The healthy way to do that is in relationships with others, where one can love and be loved, or feel importance and accomplishment, some of the most basic, instinctual human needs.

When "healthy" fails, some turn to counterfeit relationships that offer temporary comfort, but not fulfillment. Enter the drug of choice. Whenever comforted from difficult feelings by using a drug of choice, the emotional bond between pain and the solution is reinforced or strengthened. The process clinicians call "conditioning." When the bond is sufficiently strong, whenever the emotional center feels the need or emotion, an urge is sent out to indulge in the drug of choice.

If the EMS runs amuck and begins accepting counterfeit or dysfunctional solutions (the drug of choice) to meet and satisfy the needs within, and conditioning reaches the level of compulsion, the system becomes compromised. It no longer functions as intended.

"Addiction is loss of control. Addiction is the inability to predictably and consistently stop drinking, using drugs, eating, gambling, acting out sexually or other behaviors once started. Addiction is more than a behavior. Addiction starts with an emotional attachment, or relationship if you will. An emotional bond is formed to alcohol, prescription drugs, food, gambling, etc., that becomes a compulsive attachment. He or she cannot do without it. The object of the addiction becomes the best friend, lover, and the demon that will destroy the addict. Stated another way, addiction becomes a deep loss of self." (Brown)

This definition by Stephanie Brown PhD, really gets to the core of the matter when she continues: "Addiction can occur in whatever generates significant mood alteration. That means not only drugs and alcohol can be the culprits, but the self-nurturing of food, the thrill of gambling, or the arousal of sex can also initiate addiction within us. The emotional bond is formed through the conditioning process that takes place in the emotional center of our brain."

Upon continued use and (therefore) conditioning, the connection between our originating emotion and our form of acting out is strengthened and the urge becomes a compulsion. The ante has been raised at this point. At the compulsive stage of our use, we find that the urge to use is now stronger than our will to resist.

Our control of self, the ability to think and chose our reaction, has been impaired, hijacked by the emotional center. EMS has gained the ability to out-vote the thinking part of our brain. We can no longer "just say no." We have compromised our agency, and we are in trouble … big trouble. This is the beginning of our Monkey Brain's takeover.

Developing an addiction follows along this line:

Experimental	Compulsive Stage	Full-Blown Addiction
Recreational	Urge > Will to say no	We can't function without the drug.

Notes: *Each time we use or act out, we move along the addiction line and conditioning takes place. At some point, we cross into the compulsive stage. Sometimes the high is just too compelling and the process is nearly immediate.*

Patrick Carnes PhD, in his book, *Don't Call it Love*, presents the following description of the addictive process: "At some point, excessive use becomes compulsive use. The highs become so compelling that the person loses control.

"Usually the loss of control means serious consequences, yet the highs remain so compelling that the addict starts to distort, ignore or lose contact with reality. The addiction now regulates the emotional life of the addict. The addict cannot act 'normal' without the high.

"Nor can the addict deal with stressors without the maladaptive response of the addiction. The inherent shamefulness of the addict brings on self-destructive shame cycles, in which the addict's efforts to stop seem only to intensify the failures. The brain achieves a new neuro-chemical imbalance, which can only be relieved by compulsive use. The addict ends up isolated and alienated."

This is where our Monkey Brain (read "neuro-chemical imbalance") really comes to life, highs remain so compelling that the addict starts to distort, ignore, or lose contact with reality. The Monkey Brain is the source of the distortions and the logic that takes us away from reality.

Our compulsions often go against our personal values or social norms, but our EMS doesn't care about that. The EMS never considers right or wrong; it does not have a moral compass, only a mandate to find solutions to those difficult feelings. And boy, does it ever feel better to take a hit or get drunk or act out sexually or gamble or shop or eat or …

The Nature of Compulsion

George: *I am a member of a group of musicians who meet once a month to play jazz standards and top 40 songs from the 70s and 80s. It is a loose group of singers and musicians; the membership is very dynamic and constantly changing. We are generally of the same age group, ranging from 40s to 60s, male and female, from all walks of life. Our common bond is the love of the music and our desire to play with other musicians.*

Last month a new female vocalist joined the group. Let's call her Dee. She is a talented singer with an outgoing personality, attractive, in her late 40s. I did not speak to Dee during the session but did enjoy her singing as she was a marked improvement from the previous singers.

As I left the session I said my goodbyes to everyone and Dee shook my hand and said, "Nice to meet you." It seemed quite innocent but in my mind she held my hand a little longer than was required. I assumed I was making that up and promptly dismissed it.

However, it did trigger my addict's alert system, which fired up all the acting-out systems in a nanosecond. Nothing happened, but I will say I was unsettled by the incident and it planted a seed of anticipation for the next meeting.

The next session arrives and upon meeting everyone, there is an exchange of pleasantries and nothing more. Dee is there and we said, "Hi" and that was where it ended. I breathed a sigh of relief and assumed I was just making things up. I was okay with that, but my addict was clearly disappointed.

The session continued with no further contact. At quitting time I packed up my gear and said my good-byes to everyone. As I walked by Dee she stopped me, said, "Great to see you again," shaking my hand, and this time she placed her card in the palm of my hand. I left with the card not saying anything but was clearly in a state of dis-ease.

I got home and confirmed it was her card with all her contact details. Name, email, and telephone. All the warning bells went off. Not knowing what else to do I threw the card in the garbage. Great recovery behavior, but alas that is not where the story ends.

I could not stop obsessing about her. I had trouble getting to sleep, tossing and turning all night. When I woke the next morning my conscious thoughts were not much better. Among the thoughts that kept whirling through my mind were:

She couldn't possibly have meant anything by giving me her card; or did she?

Maybe she wants to get into this other band that needs a vocalist?

Maybe she is interested in me and wants to go out?

Maybe I should call her for coffee just to see what she really wants? After all, if she wants to join the band I can set up an audition. If she wants a date I will tell her I am married and not interested, what's the harm in that? (See note below on the word just and discussion in chapters 2 and 3 on brinksmanship.)

The interesting aspect of the whole thing is the card seems to be calling me from the garbage can, which is outside the house in the garage. Just like in a science fiction movie, the card took on mystical powers and is calling to me. I keep telling myself how crazy I am but cannot seem to stop the thoughts. I tried reading the paper, making breakfast, going to the coffee shop but cannot stop running the events of the evening as an endless tape recording, analyzing each second of tape, trying to decipher the meaning.

The good news is that I finally realize I am being crazy. What the scary part is that it is so easy to recognize, yet so hard to stop the crazy thoughts.

I can talk rationally to myself and say, "You did the right thing by throwing out the card." But my addict is busy in the background spinning fantasies, driving me to go pick through the garbage and get the card, with all the embarrassment and humiliation that would entail.

This is a primer on compulsive behavior and the bottom line is that compulsive behavior is deadly because it is so difficult to control. With all the skills that I have developed over my seven years of recovery this has been one of the toughest tests in the last five years. I know my Higher Power is testing me, but why does the exam have to be so hard.

So what did I do?

I called my sponsor and talked to him about it. He said, "Yes, you're crazy; no, don't call her."

I discussed this situation with my sponsees to understand how they deal with compulsive behavior. They were sympathetic and we agreed I was crazy, that it was compulsive behavior and the best thing was to do nothing.

I went to a meeting just to surround myself with serenity and recovery.

I did fish the card out of the garbage—and put it through the shredder. Dealing with compulsive behavior is the key to overcoming our addiction. If you cannot develop tools to address such situations, you are doomed to never breaking the cycle. Easy to say, incredibly difficult to do.

From the Clinic: George's experience with compulsion is instructive. The urges are strong and can be relentless. They just keep coming as the MB keeps trying to return to acting out. It will not leave the addict alone. That is the negative power of a Monkey Brain.

George went through a number of techniques to outmaneuver his MB and his addiction and not give in to making contact to see "what she really wants." He talked with his sponsor and other people, he attended meetings, and quieted himself. He used the tools of recovery, and still had a rather close call.

Here is the message in that: IT AIN'T EASY! However, gathering of the tools and learning these skills is the way to freedom from the onslaught that is coming from the Monkey Brain. As we have success, over time we will feel the power of the Monkey Brain diminish.

The Big Book of AA makes the clear point: "If you have decided you want what we have and are willing to go to any lengths to get it, then you are ready to take certain steps. At some of these we balked. We thought we could find an easier, softer way. But we could not … Some of us have tried to hold on to our old ideas and the result was nil until we let go absolutely … Half-measures availed us nothing. We stood at the turning point. Here are the steps we took, which are suggested as a program of recovery."

The Dalai Lama once made a salient point about how we use our mind. He was being interviewed by a group of American psychologists led by Dr. Daniel Brown of Harvard. The Americans were keenly interested in how His Holiness dealt with negative self-talk, a staple of the Monkey Brain condition.

The question was puzzling, the Dalai Lama spent a good deal of time with his translator trying to understand what was being asked. The problem? The idea of negative self-talk ("I am unworthy") was unfathomable to him. He finally asked, "Why would you ever let your mind get like that?"

That is a question worth asking.

The beauty of this message is that there are solutions. We Can Reclaim Our Addicted Brain! One need not be locked into Monkey Brain mode forever. Neither does one need to feel the utter despair of "hitting bottom."

There is another way.

Chapter 2

How to Grow a Monkey Brain
First, Start with an Unspoiled Brain

George: *Some old family friends established a regular get-together wherein we meet for dim sum once a month on Sunday morning. It started when their kids were in their early teens and continues even now that they in their early 30s and have kids of their own.*

Their first grandson, Jeffrey, a 24-month-old, joined us at a recent meal so we could get to know him, help socialize him, and allow him to experience a wider circle of people.

For those of you who don't know, dim sum can be a circus of activity with steam carts rolling by, servers shouting out in broken English/Chinese what they have to offer, against the background din of many simultaneous conversations. It is a mixture of sights, smells, and languages coming at you from all directions—all at the same time.

On any given Sunday morning there can be more than 250 people in this particular restaurant with a 45-minute wait to be seated, and this day was no exception.

All through the meal Jeffrey was very well-behaved. He did not seem to take to the food very much, but he sat at the table as he drank in all the sights around him. He was wide-eyed as he scanned the room. He reminded me of an owl as he turned his head to watch someone walk by, then quickly winding his head back around to see the next person as they approached. He smiled broadly and was clearly enjoying all the activity.

It brought to mind the wonders of being a child. Unbridled curiosity and interest in all things. No judgments, no prejudices, no biases. Nothing to be scared of as he looked out from the protective circle of a loving, caring family.

I watched him for a few moments, wondering what it would be like to feel like that. To be so in the moment with your environment. Then I thought to myself, "Just wait until your parents screw you up; that will all change."

Like most everything else in life, Monkey Brains don't get created in a vacuum. There are causes and constructs in play that provide fertile ground for growing a Monkey Brain.

Then Add Some Thinking Errors

The last person to know he has a Monkey Brain is the guy who has a Monkey Brain. That is the devil of it. Monkey Brains come with blindness and a complete lack of awareness of the condition. Astoundingly, most Monkey Brainers feel they are very sincere, of good intent, and are only trying to protect and reward themselves. They believe they are all-around good people. That is the reality they create for themselves. The other reality—the one the rest of us live in—escapes them.

Amy Morin, LSCW observes: "As we go about our daily routines, our internal monologue narrates our experience. Our self-talk guides our behavior and influences the way we interact with others. It also plays a major role in how you feel about yourself, other people, and the world in general.

"Quite often, however, our conscious thoughts aren't realistic; they're irrational and inaccurate. Believing our irrational thoughts can lead to problems, including communication issues, relationship problems, and unhealthy behavior decisions."

These irrational thoughts have a name, they are called 'Thinking Errors.' Thinking Errors are one type of foundation stone we use in constructing a Monkey Brain. They are created using thoughts and logic that depart from truth and reality. As the Thinking Errors proliferate in our mind, we edge closer and closer to the Monkey Brain diagnosis.

Tracy Barnhart further defines "Thinking Errors" this way: "Thinking

Errors are thoughts people exhibit or demonstrate during irresponsible behavior. This thinking leads to and brings on self-destructive behavior. This self-destructiveness leads to and brings on criminal behaviors."

A Classic Example

Right now a Monkey Brainer would be thinking: "Well, that is all well and good, but that is not me! I am not doing anything wrong or criminal and I am not going to!" Surely George felt exactly the same way just before this went down:

George: *This is a form of the old game: kick the can down the road. Or, let's keep going to see what happens and wait until we have to make decisions. I wish I could say I learned this from the government, but I perfected it long before they did.*

My therapist nicknamed this practice "brinksmanship," which was her shorthand for her meaning that I was continuing down a highly dangerous path assuming I could escape before anything disastrous occurred, when in reality I often followed it until I put myself in a box where I had to do something crazy to get out.

The technique is best described by an example. You're sitting at a bar and quietly having a drink by yourself on a Friday night before heading home after work. You're not feeling particularly good or bad, just reliving the week's events and thinking about the chores at home that are waiting to be done. You look across the bar and there is an attractive woman on the other side.

You can't tell if she is with friends or by herself but you think you noticed she was looking at you.

You think, "It can't be, you're imagining things."

You look again, and sure enough, she is looking. You make eye contact; she smiles and looks away.

Your addict brain immediately kicks in thinking: "Go for it; she's cute, available, and you haven't had any strange for a long time."

Your recovery brain says, "Three-Second Rule; look away and forget her."

Your Monkey Brain thinks, "What's so wrong with meeting someone new? She looks interesting, and a new friend can't hurt. Besides, you can stop any time; nothing will happen."

The next thing is you send over a drink, which she accepts and smiles and mouths the words, "Thank you" in your direction.

The addict brain immediately gets the adrenaline rush of the chase and it's off to the races, daring you to see if you still have what it takes.

Your recovery brain is flashing "STOP" in huge red letters.

Your Monkey Brain thinks, "She seems so nice and what's the harm in talking to her. You're just being sociable. There is nothing wrong with that. Besides, you can stop any time, nothing will happen."

Next you get a refill for your drink, take it over to where she's sitting, and sit down next to her. She smiles and makes room for you, as she introduces herself. You pour on the charm and start your well-rehearsed conversation.

Of course, you manage to skirt talking about anything real, like the fact that you're married, have two kids, a house in the suburbs, a mortgage, etc.

After another round of drinks, she asks if there isn't some place more quiet to talk.

Your addict brain is racing, getting yet another adrenaline burst thinking, "Gotcha."

Your recovery brain is flashing a bigger and brighter "STOP" sign, but the alcohol and adrenaline have pushed that out of your mind.

Your Monkey Brain is saying, "She seems so cute and nice; what's the harm in going someplace to talk. After all, you can be more "in the moment," pay closer attention to what she's saying. Besides, you can stop any time; nothing will happen."

You're now in the car, the charm is just oozing out. You say something witty and she touches your arm and moves close to nuzzle next to you.

The addict brain is pouring on the gas. The recovery brain was silenced long ago and is essentially dead.

The Monkey Brain is saying, "Go ahead, kiss her; one little kiss won't hurt. You don't want to hurt her feelings by rejecting her. And besides, you can stop any time; nothing will happen."

Of course, the next thing you know is the police are knocking on the window, pointing a high-intensity flashlight into the car, pulling you both out and arresting you for indecency in a public place, or more accurately, having sex in a public place.

But remember, you said you can stop any time!

And another Monkey Brain carries the day!

Amy Morin continues her discussion with some good news about solving the problem of Thinking Errors: "Once you recognize your thinking errors, you can begin trying to challenge those thoughts. Look for exceptions to the rule and gather evidence that your thoughts aren't 100% true. Then, you can begin replacing them with more realistic thoughts.

"The goal doesn't need to be to replace negative thoughts with overly idealistic or positive ones. Instead, replace them with realistic thoughts. Changing the way you think takes a lot of effort initially, but with practice, you'll notice big changes—not just in the way you think, but also in the way you feel and behave."

Moving away from thinking errors may not be easy. Monkey Brain recovery, while living with a Monkey Brain, can be difficult, but consider the alternative. Living a life directed by a Monkey Brain is a life spent in fantasy and flawed thinking, using a set of rules that you made up and only you understand. In other words, anti-social.

The genealogy of the Monkey Brain formation always includes a healthy collection of thinking error ancestors.

Sample Genres of Thinking Errors

Teenage/Criminal Thinking. Teenagers have something of an excuse: their brains aren't fully developed—they create Thinking Errors by the bucketful. The logic trail they follow may have some very valid moments intermingled with logic jumps, and half-truths are the rule rather than the exception.

"But, Mom, everyone's doing it," ignores truth, reality, and family moral values while having a very compelling feel, except of course, for mothers. Mothers know "everyone" is a thinking error of the generalization and over-simplification genre. Mothers know it is a rare day when "everyone" acts in unison about anything.

Mothers know the popularity of an activity is insufficient cause for participating.

Mom often replies, "If they jumped off a bridge, would you follow them?" Which generates this reaction: "Of course not, don't be ridiculous. This is nothing like that," illustrating the Monkey Brainer's myopic view of his world.

Thinking errors foster rationalizations and justifications and are the fuel of the Monkey Brain fire. The logic of: "The bank has insurance; they won't lose any money if I rob them" fills prisons. Truly, among inmates there are few guilty convicts. The Monkey Brain techniques upon which they base their thinking frees them from responsibility. They feel no guilt because of their sense of entitlement coming from the perception of being wronged.

The Black-and-White Variety. Some are fond of black-and-white thinking, an all-or-nothing approach to life and reasoning. Things are either good or bad, a success or failure; there is no middle ground or any gray areas. Since life contains acres and acres of gray, a reality built that does not includes gray areas has some very big holes in it.

Over-Generalizers. Over-generalizing is the foundation of many thinking errors. Racial tensions are often supported by this over-generalization: "All (white, black, yellow, red) people are lazy (or whatever degrading word fits)."

"None of the other kids have to" has been a favorite argument for many generations.

Another example would be: "Everybody fudges on their taxes." While certainly true for a portion of the population, it is not the reality of all taxpayers. Making blanket statements based on partial truths is the core of over-generalizations and makes the Monkey Brain feel safe.

The Glass Is Half Empty. Some seem to disregard any positive information. The performer who makes a small error, unnoticed by the audience, feels his effort was awful. Some people have never experienced a good day because each day contains some moment that did not go particularly well and they cannot keep themselves from focusing on that moment and ignoring all that was positive. Pervasive pessimism is fertile ground for growing thinking errors.

Mind Readers. Some thinking error victims think they are mind readers. They don't bother with facts or asking for clarification instead, they assume. They fill in the blanks themselves without considering things as they really are. This feeling often hangs out with the "I am the smartest person in the room" syndrome.

George: *People at work frequently got mad at me because I had a habit of finishing their sentences for them. I thought I showed empathy for what they were saying as well as that I was a quick study, catching on quickly to what they were talking about. Instead they found it annoying. It made them feel like I wasn't really listening to them and that I was trying to show off how smart I was.*

Makers of Catastrophe. Some are certain doom is upon us. They love the chaos. Chaos creates a comfort. Not content with the reality of their lives, or perhaps lacking the skills to live in the world as it is, they often create chaos, especially if none is on its way naturally. The feeling of imminent or future catastrophe can be dysfunctionally empowering.

Of course, don't forget the victim card. It is impossible to assume the victim stance without these thinking errors. What better way to elicit the call for rescue than to create a nice little catastrophe.

These folks love "future trippin." If a catastrophe isn't on today's horizon they will go out into the future to find one. John is an example, a college student in his sophomore year, he was having trouble getting to class and doing well in his studies. Some clinical investigation determined he was immobilized by depression and fear of failing the required testing for entering medical school—a test he would not take for three years.

Thinking Errors and Denial

When building a Monkey Brain, thinking errors can be very helpful to employ the truth and reality-bending benefits of denial. Denial is the hall pass to addiction. Denial is the tool our Monkey Brain uses to either justify acting out or hide it completely, especially from our own eyes. Some of the hardest work of addiction recovery is recognizing, coming to terms with, and gaining freedom from the patterns of denial created by our Monkey Brain.

Unfortunately, we lie to ourselves as much as we lie to others. "I need this," or "No one will know," even "I am not hurting anyone." The list of thinking errors from denial is very long. Addicts are very creative people. Often, the more intelligent they are, the more magnificent the Monkey Brain they can create and the greater difficulty getting into and staying in recovery.

Minimizing and Absolute Denial

The Monkey Brain loves absolute denial: "I am NOT that guy!" He also throws in a little minimizing for good measure: "Yes, I had some problems with affairs, but I am not a sex addict." (This after a dozen or so affairs outside of his marriage.)

Addicts minimize the impact of their acting out on themselves or others. They convince themselves they act out infrequently and as a result it is not really a problem. "I only go to the strip club on Friday nights." "I only see a prostitute twice a month, so it's no big deal."

Often they will add that they can stop any time they want, so it is all under control. Of course, they cannot and rarely stop without intervention from a higher power, which can be legal, familial or spiritual.

Alternatively, they convince themselves that their acting out is victimless, such as prostitution or compulsive masturbation. In their minds, there is nothing wrong with what they are doing since no one is hurt or, in the case of prostitution, they make up that they are really in love or are supporting the prostitute in some altruistic fantasy.

Both of these are flawed thinking, which to the addict mind (Monkey Brain) is perfectly rational.

One of the classic reasons individuals cannot recognize themselves as addicts is that they don't meet their definition or their mind's picture of what an addict is. It is the perfect setup for minimizing:

Elton was a high-functioning alcoholic. He taught high school, didn't miss work, and was very well-respected by both colleagues and students. In Elton's mind, an alcoholic was the guy in that Christmas movie with Jimmy Stewart. The unshaven guy, disheveled, stumbling in and out of bars, begging for money or drinks. Elton was nothing like that, so there was no way he could convict himself of being a drunk.

Reality is that alcoholics come in all kinds of packages, and Elton came to understand this when he was driving home from work with a very high blood/alcohol content and was the cause of a terrible accident that took someone's life.

He couldn't deny that he was a drunk anymore.

An extreme example of absolute denial is given by an undercover agent on Clark County Washington's Drug Task Force:

"If we are following a car with marijuana, cocaine or heroin, as soon as we are discovered, windows come down and drugs fly out the window; however, meth users believe they won't be found out even if they are stopped by police.

"Once I pulled over a meth guy and got him out of the car. I asked, 'Do you have any drugs on you?'

"He answered instantly and emphatically, 'No!'

"When I searched his pants, and found a stash, he blurted out, 'These aren't my pants!'

"Now my first question upon stopping a suspect is, 'Uhh, are those your pants?'"

Monkey Brainers that use meth can really bend reality with denial. Their drug of choice profoundly harms the brain, creating a surge of thinking errors. The thinking and denial patterns progress to a point of being so distorted and illogical that anyone else can easily recognize the lie. The meth addict doesn't get it and thinks he is believable.

The addict is able to ignore flashing lights, the police presence, believing he will talk his way out of trouble. He is quite indignant when we can't accept his explanation. This is absolute denial on steroids!

The meth addict is so trapped in his thinking that getting out of that mind-world is impossible without a great deal of help. Help that he doesn't see as necessary. The culmination for the meth user is paranoia. Constant fear and vigilance because "those guys over there are after me."

It's not uncommon to hear a heavy drug-user minimize by saying, "No way I'm an addict. I don't use needles." Monkey Brain logic for sure. It keeps the addict in the "What I am doing is not that bad!" category. And it allows the escape from the reality of whom we have become.

Monkey Brainers love to use anger and indignation as a first line of defense and an alternative to things like honesty, integrity, fairness, compassion or admitting their addictions. In their confusion, many spouses and friends, hurt and fearful, back down from the angry, bellowing addict. Being loud and angry doesn't change anything. If you're using a Monkey Brain, you've entered a new world, living in a different reality doesn't make you right, no matter how loud you bellow.

Denial by Avoidance

A Monkey Brain avoider is happy to talk about anything that does not involve his addiction or harmful behaviors. He has become an expert at manipulation to keep the spotlight off himself. He uses a variety of techniques to practice his form of denial.

He is great at changing the focus by asking provocative questions that put attention on others. He loves to put others down and gets a double payoff: it makes him feel better about himself, and it focuses attention away from his use.

He might say, "So, I saw the cops over at your house last week … what was going on?"

Or, "John said you weren't at the AA meeting last night and he thought you were out drinking instead … so what's going on?"

This technique brings on a harvest of self-righteousness and superiority that is very satisfying to the Monkey Brain.

Users of avoidance become masters at being vague. I guess … Maybe … I have one or two, tops! … I drink socially … I smoke occasionally is the flavor of their conversations. They are purposefully unspecific and unclear to avoid others knowing their reality. Monkey Brainers really buy into this pattern, believing with all their heart it is true.

Avoiders may also like to create drama. They love to keep things stirred up—always at the expense of others. The benefit is again creating a smoke screen that helps hide their own behaviors and situation from public knowledge.

George: *Before I got into recovery, my wife swore I was addicted to chaos. Of course I never saw it. She called me a whirling dervish that would create chaos where none existed. In recovery I learned that I was an adrenaline junkie and needed the chaos to get a fix. If things were quiet, I would feel uncomfortable, irritable, as if I was going through withdrawal. So to medicate I looked for places to create chaos so I could get a fix.*

Denial by Rationalization

This Monkey Brainer always has a good reason. Excuses were created for rationalizers: "I drink because I'm depressed." "Pot is the only thing that relieves the pain." Rationalizers punch their own ticket to get on the addiction train. They rationalize themselves right into trouble.

Good rationalizers can be quite convincing and have enough truth and logic that we accept what they say without question. Individuals of high intellect are especially good at this form of denial.

George: *My therapist told me to be on the lookout for situations when I use the word "just" to make a crazy idea seem reasonable. In her thinking, whatever surrounded the word "just" was a rationalization about to happen, whose sole* *purpose was to make me feel okay doing something that was at best crazy and at worst very harmful. Accordingly, I learned that if I used the word "just" in a sentence I needed to put on the brakes—hard.*

For example, once I was curious about how an old girlfriend was doing, so I called her "just" to make sure she was okay. I sent another ex-girlfriend an email "just" to make sure she was all right. I spent a few hours on Facebook looking up old acting-out partners "just" to make sure they were okay.

I noticed the word coming into my thinking often. It is a form of rationalization, which as I mentioned previously, makes it acceptable to kick the can down the road, thus pushing my behavior to the edge, to the point where I either had to retreat (which usually was not an option) or go over the cliff. These are very dangerous situations, increasing the likelihood of a slip or a fall. So the key is to recognize them and go the other way.

What is really educational for me now that I work with sponsees is the number of times I hear them use the same "Just-ifications" to rationalize their acting-out. Once your ear gets used to listening for it, I think you will surprise yourself how often you do it.

So endeth the lesson.

Denial by Blaming

The Monkey Brain that plays the blame game has never been at fault for anything. There is always someone or something else to blame. Blamers create resentment to their advantage. "Your nagging is impossible to live with … who wouldn't drink?"

By creating a victim role for themselves, they feel justified in medicating/using. Friends of addicts can reinforce these feelings, sometimes without knowing it. They can do this by supporting the addict's assertions ("Yes, your wife is being unreasonable") or by not saying anything.

Rarely will they say, "I think you have a problem." Primarily because people feel sympathy for a victim. We want to be good friends, supportive, empathetic, nice people. Blamers use this to their advantage and set us up. Making us feel just enough sympathy for them that we do not question their solutions.

Denial by Comparing

Those that compare are close cousins to the minimizers. They take comfort in the fact that they aren't as bad as "that" guy. They often take the next step in logic and deduce for themselves that they are not addicts.

John's brother was in and out of rehab most of his adult life. He couldn't keep a job or a relationship; he seemed unable to shake the demons. John spent a great deal of time and money trying to help his brother. John was highly respected at work and everyone said he had a beautiful family, so it never occurred to him that he was also an alcoholic. Yes, he was drinking a fifth a day, but he didn't have the problems his brother did.

Comparing sounds like this: "Yeah, I use some, but I'm not out of control; I'm sure not like that tweaked-out Jerry. Now that guy has a problem. You should be talking to him!" The addict is very comforted that he is not Jerry, even to the point that he can completely excuse his own addiction as not that bad. This isn't very far from, "I do not have a problem."

George: *My first real effort to get into recovery was attending a week-long men's session in an expensive rehab center. I thought I was going in for alcoholism but instead got put in with a group of men who were sex addicts. Apparently I had tipped my hand unknowingly during intake.*

There were six of us and I was the third one to tell my story. The first fellow told us how he attached little mirrors to his shoes so he could position his feet to look up women's dresses. If he found someone in provocative underwear, he liked to spit on them. The fellow right before me was a disbarred attorney who was living on the street and prostituted himself to get money for drugs and alcohol.

Then it was my turn and I said, "I know I am really screwed up, but I am nowhere near as bad as these guys … I mean come on." The counselor gave me a stern look and said, "From where I sit, you are just as bad as they are. You may have taken different roads to get here, but you are here and now getting into recovery is what it's all about." I turned 40 shades of red, some from anger, some from embarrassment, and I told my story. As much as I hated to admit it, she was 100% right.

"I Am Better; Therefore, I Am Well" Denial

There is a phenomenon in recovery that creates a denial pattern. When recovery is begun with some sincerity, progress is made. There are immediate results that are noticed by the addict doing the work. Clarity begins to return, guilt and shame are eased, and the addict feels better than they have felt for some time.

After this, it is easy for the Monkey Brain to believe that healing has happened and is accomplished. Incorrectly then, they believe they can reintroduce old acting-out behaviors with little or no risk. The Monkey Brain asserts that their using wasn't that bad and is certain they can use on a limited basis without harm. Those who fall into this trap are soon back in their addictive behaviors, many times deeper than they were before.

Denial by Hopelessness

Hopelessness is a constant companion in many Monkey Brains. You can only try to quit an addiction so many times without success before the belief is formed that quitting is not possible. Giving up hope soon follows. When hope is lost, the Monkey Brain's game has moved to a whole new level, and recovery becomes much more difficult. Even reaching out or seeking help becomes impractical in the Monkey Brain.

Addicts affected by hopelessness can allow themselves unlimited involvement in their addiction. After all, there is nothing that can be done. The deduction of their best thinking becomes, "This is my fate."

George: *I remember having this discussion with my first CSAT therapist. I asked her if addressing my sex addiction was impossible as it was in my DNA. I knew my father was a sex addict and assumed my brother was one too, so I was wondering if what I was trying to do was impossible. "You can't fight DNA" is often cited around the house whenever my wife or I say or do something exactly as our parents would.*

What I didn't think of, which my therapist quickly called me on, was that if she said, "Yes, it could not be addressed" that I would use that as a blank check to act out as often as I liked. I had a ready-made excuse: I can't help it; I am genetically driven to be a womanizer! For those who think you cannot change, all I can say is you're wrong. If you are rigorously honest and are willing to change, you can change.

Denial by Right

This Monkey Brainer recognizes what he is doing, admits his addiction, but claims the right to continue his self-destruction. "I have the right to kill myself! Leave me alone!" It is a very common denial pattern among adolescent males and is often founded on anger and shame.

Jimi Hendrix wrote, "I'm the one who dies when it's time for me to die, so let me live my life the way I want to." (If 6 Was 9; Axis Bold As Love). What most addicts fail to consider when they are in this paradigm is the impact of their decisions on others. It is ironic, but killing yourself is the ultimate selfish act.

George: *Every February I mourn the death of my college roommate. He committed suicide after being indicted for a crime he did not commit. He killed himself as he could not face the scrutiny and embarrassment of being indicted. I was completely unaware of his passing for several months until a mutual friend told me about it after finding newspaper articles on the event. I immediately thought, "Why didn't you reach out to anyone? Why didn't you call me? We could have talked and maybe you would still be alive."*

Then a harsh realization hit me. I had tried the same thing almost on the exact day. Instead of a gun, I used painkillers, sleeping pills, and a fifth of gin. Of course, I reached out to no one, alone with my pain and self-loathing. Every year I remind myself what is and what could have been had I been successful in my attempt.

Accountability Is the Only Known Antidote for Denial

(Please see chapter 3 for the discussion of Accountability.)

George: *Being committed to your recovery means you know what you have to do and you actually do it (what a concept!). Not act out, work the steps, go to meetings, help others, etc. You know where the boundaries are, and you stay inside them so you can be sober and gain serenity. You do what you say you will do and are rigorously honest about yourself and your actions. Seems very straightforward and it is; however, when you look for examples of this in action in society you see quite the opposite at work.*

As a general rule we say one thing and do another.

To prove my point of view I will use two divergent examples: the practice of religion and speeding. Very different things, I know, but bear with me.

Think for a moment about how many people practice religion and how they actually live their lives. They go to church every week but do they actually "do unto others as they would have them to unto themselves." Sometimes that "level of spirituality" doesn't even make it out of the parking lot.

I live across the street from a church and believe me you don't want to be on the street when Sunday mass gets out. You take your life in your hands if you are on the street driving or walking. People are in a competition to get out of the parking lot to get to Starbucks first—so much for brotherly love.

I was raised Jewish and once I completed my Bar Mitzvah, we stopped going to temple. I was very confused by this as up until that big event we went to services every Friday night and I attended various religious tutoring and social functions. The big event comes and goes and we stop going to temple. The only time we set foot in the door after that was for the high holy days. I thought this was very hypocritical, but I was told to mind my own business and keep my thoughts to myself. What I learned from this was it was fine to do one thing for the benefit/consumption of others and something quite different for yourself.

I think this helped set me up for my addiction as I realized you could live life with a double standard. As a matter of fact, you actually needed to have a double life to be a productive member of society. So I maintained two lives, at a minimum, one for my wife, family and friends, and another for my addict, which had a vastly different set of values. So in my circle of friends, I would condemn extramarital affairs even though I may have been having one at the very moment.

I raise this issue as I believe it is part of the reason some people have such a hard time gaining traction in their recovery. They cannot see good behavior in action in society. Instead, we have been raised in an environment where it is perfectly acceptable to "not practice what you preach." It's okay for the other guy, but I don't have to do this or that. So when we are asked to be rigorously honest and to live a life of integrity, we sign up and then proceed to look for shortcuts or look for an easy way out. I hate to be the bearer of bad news, but in recovery there is no easy way out. Recall that the 12 Steps are simple; no one ever said they were easy.

My second example is highway speed limits. I live in a large city in the south where most of the posted speed limits on the highway are 60 or 65 mph. Having said that, if you're on the road and not doing 80 mph, you will get run down by traffic.

In addition, there are radar traps all over, which I know from my own experience, but you can still sail through at 80 mph and not get pulled over. Which leads me to ask the question: What is the speed limit really? What is the expectation of society? How are we expected to conduct our lives? Is it what is on the sign, or is it what everyone does? And if everyone does it, is it okay even though the law says otherwise? In other words, we say one thing and do another on the road every day.

Here is a situation I used to use at work when lecturing on business ethics: read it and think hard about how you would handle it.

You go to your regular supermarket to buy groceries. The bill is $175 and you give the clerk two $100 dollar notes. The clerk makes change and hands you back too much money. How much does it have to be before you tell the cashier they made an error? $1, $5, $10, more? Or would you never tell them and just pocket the excess?

This is a litmus test of how well you can do what is required when no one is watching. What you do in the confines of your own mind is an integral part of recovery. How far are you willing to push the envelope? The amount is different for each of us, but this little test provides some good insight into your inner voice *and what you might do when no one is looking.*

This line of thinking is very problematic for addicts. Addicts are experts in double standards and have a PhD in knowing how to maintain multiple personas. Even when the rules are clear, they look for shortcuts. So the society in which we live teaches us how it is acceptable not to be honest.

My advice is: don't be afraid to buck conventional wisdom and exercise good self-care by using rigorous honesty.

"Recovery progress must be measured in terms of behavior and not words. Monkey Brainers are masters of word manipulation. Words can easily paint any picture we wish. That is why denial serves the addict's purpose. Behaviors reveal the true intention of the heart. Whether with ourselves or those with whom we are trying to rebuild relationships, don't listen to the words. Watch the behaviors.

"It is easy to say, I am no longer going to lie to you. The truth and the reality will be revealed over time, as honesty is displayed repeatedly and dishonesty is absent.

'But he said he had changed' are the most often uttered words of spouses who have been disappointed, yet again.

"The words alone of an addict cannot be trusted. Only consistent, reliable behavior can be believed." (The Waterfall Concept)

Denial patterns are presented when the client uses his addict voice. "I am not as bad as John." "I don't have a problem." "I am past help." The raising of the addict's voice is a very important therapeutic moment. The clinician has opportunity to further recovery by pointing out these statements and identifying them:

"That is your Monkey Brain speaking."

At this moment the client may be introduced to the addict within, a meeting that is often quite surprising.

Some Other Factors for Creating Monkey Brains

Poor Emotional Management Skills

News Flash! Our emotions often take us into a new reality of our own making. We may make judgments out of our anger, resentment, or embarrassment. The negative emotions always filter out reality to let in only the "facts" that justify our hurt. That makes generating some really great thinking errors easy.

George: *I know I have poor emotional management skills. It is something I'm working on all the time. Here is an example of how my mind works against me, sometimes in a fraction of a second. As part of my normal morning ritual, I am getting ready for work. I've taken a shower, and I am at the bathroom sink getting ready to put in my contact lenses as I do every morning.*

Opening the case, I get the right lens out and proceed to put the lens in my right eye. I blink once or twice and realize the lens is not there.

Looking around the sink area, I can't find it. I check the countertop, moving everything around. Nothing. Check the floor; no lens. Then my monologue starts.

"Damn it, I don't have time for this now; I don't want to be late; the morning traffic will be a nightmare. Why on a Monday morning?"

A quick second search of the countertop again reveals nothing. I get on my hands and knees on the floor, carefully feeling across the floor for the lens. Still nothing. The thoughts continue.

"I better call the optometrist because it will take me at least a week to get an appointment. Then a week to get the lens; then I am backed up against the wall because I leave for vacation right after that. Gee, I hope it comes in on time. I would hate to be using my old lenses on this trip because the prescription is so

old I can't see out of them.

"Come to think of it, I dropped my insurance, so it is going to cost me. That's something I don't need right before I go away.

"Damn, it's getting late and I can just feel the traffic building outside the house ... where is that stupid thing. What a klutz I am."

I take a deep breath to calm myself.

"Okay, I KNOW it's here ... it has to be."

The search begins anew, a little less careful and a little more desperate this time. Now I'm perspiring as the anxiety permeates my metabolism. I look in the mirror and a new monologue begins.

"You ass. You always do this. You always lose something right before vacation and scramble around trying to fix it before you leave. Why can't you be more careful? You are such an idiot; you never catch a break."

I look at myself in the mirror with a look of disdain at what I see. Then I realize the lens is stuck precariously to my eyebrow. It had been there all along and I never saw it. If you need an example of the power and insanity of self-talk, there you go.

Taking Things Personally

George: *Another way to think of this is asking the question, "How good am I at boundaries?" I've heard in many a session that to deal with certain issues you need a black belt in boundaries. While I understood the concept, the practice of boundaries is much more challenging.*

Essentially there are two types of boundaries, "protective" and "containment" (per Pia Melody).

Protective boundaries protect you as the name implies, keeping things out that you don't want. Containment boundaries keep "you" from spilling out into the world.

For most of my life I didn't have any protective boundaries. By this I mean I took everything anyone ever said about me personally, assuming it was true, taking it in as a criticism at face value.

I can recall when I was five years old one of the most devastating comments

I heard from a friend: "You tie your shoes like a Jew." It is some 60 years later and I can remember that event like it was yesterday. Clearly no good boundaries at work there.

I can also remember people making fun of my clothes, that I was overweight, the way I spoke, my lack of ability in sports, that I took school seriously, etc. etc. I was called a Momma's boy and routinely beat up. All of this led me to question who I was and why people hated me so much. It must be me! After all they can't all be mistaken. I so desperately wanted to be accepted by everyone but didn't know what I was doing wrong. I had few friends and felt isolated most of the time. Quite a bit of trauma there.

By the same token, my containment boundaries worked overtime. I never let anything out. When I was mad, sad, etc., I just bottled it up and kept it all inside. My family was such that if I said anything, I was criticized for being weak or not being a man. After all, men deal with their issues: they don't cry about them.

The pressure built up to such a level that I had ulcers by age 16. Years later I described this to my therapist saying I felt like a bottle of warm soda, shaken vigorously and then slammed on the table. We all know what happens in that case. The contents foam up and pressure inside reaches critical levels until it is either released or dissipates. Mine was never released or dissipated. Instead it was stored until I was old enough to embark on my addictions. Is it any wonder that I was an alcoholic from my first drink or a sex addict from my first encounter with a woman?

What I learned in recovery is that your protective boundaries act as a gateway. You can keep out the things you don't want and allow in the things you do want. Of course, you can block all information or only accept the information you like, but that is a different kind of emotional disorder.

Discerning what to let in and what to keep out is how you develop your black belt in boundaries. Perceptions of what to let in change over time but it is safe to say that not everything you hear should come in and not everything that comes in requires a reaction on your part.

A simple example of a containment boundary is when someone wrongs you and you think, "I'd like to murder that S-O-B." Most of us don't actually go through with it. Those who don't have effective containment boundaries in place might. We use containment boundaries to show proper emotions at the proper time, being vulnerable when appropriate, or not making jokes at a funeral.

As I said, I used to keep everything bottled up. That is until I started drinking. Then everything came out. My containment boundaries disappeared and I would say some of the cruelest things to family, friends, and total strangers. So much so that I would spend the days after a binge avoiding people for fear that I had insulted them in some way. I would feel so bad afterwards that I would build stronger boundaries and keep everything in until the next time I binged. Then watch out.

I heard that I was considered by coworkers, friends, and family to be like a land mine—you never knew when you might step in the wrong place and I'd go off like an explosion.

Medicating

George: *How is it possible that the addict doesn't recognize the insanity, the development of the Monkey Brain. Essentially because it starts small and ramps up.*

Stories of addiction vary, but they generally follow the same theme. A medicating behavior is tried (sex, drugs, alcohol) and provides the desired high. The addict wants to repeat that feeling and tries again, but the high is not as good as the first time.

At this point they add more fuel, increasing the acting-out behavior. Two drinks a night becomes four, eight, then 16. Going to the strip club once a month becomes once a week and then every day. It doesn't matter what the choice of drug is, the process is always the same.

What differs is how quickly it will ramp up and become unmanageable. Sometimes it can be over several years, other times over several months, weeks, or even days. The acting-out behavior starts small and then grows until something catastrophic occurs, i.e., hit bottom.

Some folks have high bottoms and can maintain many aspects of a normal life; they are able to keep a job, marriage, friends, etc. Others have low bottoms and wind up losing everything, on occasion even their lives.

You can liken it to the recipe for drunken prawns. Drunken prawns are prepared by taking live prawns and putting them in a pot of room temperature wine. The prawns are quite content in their new environment and start to get drunk. Turning the heat up, the temperature slowly rises until the wine boils.

The resulting prawns are tender and delicious. Unlike throwing live prawns in a pot of boiling water, they don't tense up and fear for their lives.

Addiction grows in much the same way, starting small and growing in intensity—until you are dinner.

Entitlement

George: *Acting from a sense of entitlement is a powerful motivation and can lead us to do just about anything. It manifests itself in many ways. It can be a reward for hard work, a reward for putting up with something you don't like, a reward for being misunderstood, being alone, or even a reward for being one-down. Have you ever felt you deserved to act out because _____ (fill in the blank)?*

Answers could include: my wife doesn't understand me, I had a bad day at work, I had a good day at work, etc. Acting from this position is very dangerous for addicts as our boundaries are down and our pleasure center needs are up.

I heard this expression at an AA meeting that sums up one sense of entitlement: "Poor me, poor me, pour me a drink!"

Here is another, which is just as crazy. I have a sponsee who never makes it past 30 days of sobriety. He figures that once he has been sober for four weeks he deserves a reward. So he acts out. Then he feels shame and remorse and doubles his efforts until he is sober for 30 days, then he acts out again. The prescription in this case: act out, sober up, act out, repeat until dead.

One way to turn the sense of entitlement around and have it work for you is to change your paradigm by thinking sobriety is the reward (instead of acting out). That is usually the last place we addicts go: that sobriety is a reward. It seems to be more a punishment. But if you can get there, it can be a powerful motivator.

My own story is that I was a hard-working, successful professional who enjoyed the rewards of my efforts. I had a nice house and car and a beautiful wife. I took great vacations, traveled the world, etc. Yet I felt my life was empty and unsatisfying. Often I was so depressed I contemplated suicide many times and attempted it twice. Before I got into recovery, I had numerous affairs with married and single women, each of which left me feeling empty and exhausted once the initial excitement wore off.

My addict mind told me I deserved to act out. It was my reward and I earned it. I worked hard, gave my wife everything she wanted, and put up with all of the bad things in my life without a peep. In therapy I revealed that "I deserve to act out. My wife doesn't love me the way I want and my boss doesn't treat me the way I want, so I deserve something for all that. I act out because I am entitled after all the sacrifices I made for work and my wife."

After several years working my recovery, I had an epiphany. I repositioned my view on acting-out behavior and realized it was doing the opposite of what I wanted. It was not fulfilling or satisfying me. Instead it was draining me, making me depressed and angry. I realized what I deserved were not false benefits of acting out but the true benefits of being sober. This paradigm shift changed how I looked at life. I felt entitled to be sober, not be an addict, and behaved accordingly. Suddenly I "got the program" and dedicated myself to recovery and living a healthy lifestyle.

Here is another way entitlement shows up, in a non-addict story.

We were visiting some friends who recently became grandparents. Much of the conversation centered on their new grandson and how wonderful he is. Noticing that grandma seemed a little depressed, I inquired what was wrong. She told me, "His mother (her daughter-in-law) won't allow him to stay overnight with us. She also doesn't want us to have strangers in the house when he is with us. I am really angry at her insensitivity."

Being curious, I asked, "Why are you angry?"

She responded, "He's my grandson and I'm entitled to have him stay over or take care of him whatever way I want. I've raised two kids and they turned out just fine. Who does she think she is telling me what to do?"

As soon as she said, "I'm entitled," alarm bells started going off in my head. Knowing grandma's agitated state, I asked sheepishly, "Don't you think you are overstepping your bounds a little bit? She is the mother and she can set whatever care standards for her child she sees fit. If that means no overnight stays or strangers in the house until he's older that seems reasonable to me."

I went on and said the fact that she is not raising her son the way you raised your kids is not her problem. "While I understand how you feel, I think you may want to dial it back a few notches and let go." This did little more than to make grandma angrier. In an effort to keep the peace, we moved on to a different subject.

What struck me about this event was how strong her feelings were and how adamant she was about her position and the flawed thinking that got her there. There was no talking to her and certainly no middle ground in her mind. She was entitled. No ifs, ands or buts. What was perfectly rational and sane to her was crazy to the rest of us.

It made me realize just how crazy I was when I was in my addiction and acting out from a sense of entitlement. Once in that mode of thinking, an addict can justify most behaviors. All at the manipulation of the Monkey Brain.

The Stance of a Victim

George: *It's no coincidence that I would grow up trying to control everything and everyone in my life. I was an addict and that is what addicts do. Early in life, I learned that love was conditional, and in order to stay loved I had to meet what I thought were the expectations of the ones I wanted to be loved by, mostly my mother and father.*

I also assumed everyone operated the same way, that their love was conditional and as such I had to make sure I said only what they wanted to hear. I assumed that if they heard the truth—knew the real me—they would never stay. I was just like any good politician who spins their message for each new audience.

I assumed that the truth would do anything but set me free. Accordingly, I developed a set of truths (or lies if you prefer) for each group of people in my life. To my friends, I was one person (a hard-drinking bad boy), to my teachers another (serious student who was quiet in class and did his homework), to my parents yet another (did what I was told and stayed out of sight). To do this, one has to have a very good memory (which I don't) and must supply just enough "facts" for people to stay but not so many that they will leave.

I gravitated towards "control" positions as I grew older. I became a certified public accountant and my professional expertise was in operational control systems of all kinds, writing procedures and policies for my employer. I was such a natural at them that I made it my profession.

One thing I was convinced of was that if I was honest and told the truth—particularly about how I felt—no one would like me, let alone love me, and I would be alone. Being alone was my biggest fear. So, I became a master at half-truths and never really told anyone what was actually going on inside my head.

The hardest thing for me in recovery was to let go and let God. It was particularly hard to tell the truth and let others make the decisions they wanted based on that truth. Letting go of outcomes is not something we do naturally. I was convinced everyone would leave if they knew the truth.

Amazingly, they didn't.

The Need to Control

George: *Feeling the victim is like feeling that all or part of the world is against you. No matter what you do, you are not appreciated for your efforts. Sometimes this occurs at work; sometimes it involves relatives, friends, spouse, etc.*

I have a shorthand for this: "you don't love me the way I want you to," to which I usually add some graphic instruction of what you can do to yourself.

This feeling of being one-down, less-than, not good enough, etc. is very toxic and can lead us to want to medicate. We feel trapped because in our minds we cannot leave the situation. Be it our jobs or relationships, we feel trapped. And because of that, we feel helpless and become hopeless and want to act out. What this mind-set fails to recognize is that implicit in our situation we made a choice to stay. If we are unhappy about the situation, do something about it. If you stay, you shouldn't complain. It is a conscious act to continue in the status quo.

In my work career, many of my coworkers and I often felt trapped by the company's draconian employee relations policies. What we did was go to work and complain all day long, feeling miserable because we were not appreciated. We even had an acronym for this, POPO, or passed-over and pissed-off.

However, few of us ever thought of leaving to look for another job. We assumed, and probably rightly so, that we would not make as much money working for another company and did not want to start over again. So we felt victimized by our own decision to stay. We felt trapped because that was how we felt. In reality we were not trapped at all. So, to address this we need to move out of the position of the victim.

My wife and I took a long-awaited road trip from Houston, Texas, to Park City, Utah, where we planned to spend the month of June. The trip plan included stops in some national parks along the way. We were traveling with our aging dog, so we were limited in where we could stay and what amenities were offered.

This was spring of 2012. If that does not ring a bell with you, that was the time when forest fires were spreading their way from Texas to Montana. What is more, there was a regional heat wave for several weeks where the daytime temperatures were over 100 degrees.

We set out early in the morning and got stuck in a massive traffic jam in Dallas, delaying us three hours. The next day we are in the car for some 12 hours, trying to make up for lost time. As we are about to roll into Durango where we planned to stay the night, the highway patrol flags us down and stops us. The road is blocked due to the fires crossing the highway. This caused us to make a 100-mile detour, spending more than 15 hours in the car, with the dog!

At this point I felt like God had it out for me. What did I do to deserve this? Especially on a trip we had been looking forward to and had planned so carefully for so long.

The next day we had planned to visit a national park, which is closed due to the fires. We could see the helicopters hovering over the lake, picking up water to dump on the fires next to the highway. After a night in a fleabag hotel (and I do not exaggerate there), we decided to forgo all of the other stops and push on to Park City.

We got to Park City and arrived at the house we'd rented. It was a friend's place who was going away for the month, so we got a good deal on the rental. What we did not know was the house had no air-conditioning and the bed in the master bedroom was a twin (since the owner is a single woman).

At that point, I'm wondering what else can go wrong.

We unpack the car, get the dog settled, and do some shopping. Later we go to a local gym to check out the facilities. We get back to the car to see that it was hit in the rear end and the rear driver's side door. Not once, but twice! To make matters worse, the car was only three months old at the time.

We went out to dinner with some friends and I was fuming. I'm ranting about the weather, the house, the lack of consideration of Park City drivers, and on and on. So much so that my wife was actually scared I would have a heart attack.

After a few days of steaming and stewing, I called my therapist since I knew these feelings were not good for my sobriety and my wife was ready to toss me to the curb.

My therapist listened to my tirade. And as they often do, she said, "Uh-huh, I see, yes, yes, I understand." All of which does little to improve my mood. She then asked, "Do you have your Visa card with you?"

I said yes, not understanding what that had to do with anything.

The she said, "Look, you have every right to your feelings. And what is more, if you are unhappy where you are, you have the right to leave. You don't have to stay where you are so miserable. Take your Visa card, call the airline, book a flight to Houston and get out of there. Your wife and the dog can stay as long and drive back whenever they want. You don't have to be there if you don't want to be, especially if it is making you so miserable. Just leave!"

I sat there in stunned silence. I thought about this for a few minutes and it was like someone had lifted a weight off my chest. Indeed, I had options that I never considered. I was not a prisoner; I did not have to stay in the non-air-conditioned house with the small bed. I could leave any time I wanted. Suddenly I was no longer a victim. It changed my paradigm completely with one sentence.

That was enough for me to stop the runaway thoughts in my head and to calm down. I agreed to think about it overnight and make a decision by the end of the next day. That was enough for me to start thinking rationally again and realize that "bad" things had happened, but they were not directed at me personally and they were beyond my control. The only thing in my control was what I did in response.

As it turned out, I stayed the entire month and had a great time. On the return trip, we visited all of the parks that we had to skip on the way north.

And I stayed sober.

Arriving at the Scene of the Accident

The creation of a Monkey Brain often has some profound underpinnings. Certain life experiences or circumstances greatly improve our chances of forming a Monkey Brain. Understanding these components is also a key piece of recovery. They dictate portions of our recovery plan. If these are present in our history, therapeutic resolution is advised. Just as a medical doctor would search for the diagnosis that fits the presenting symptoms, understanding how we arrived at addiction helps us formulate treatment and determine the way out of it.

(Note the reader: As you read this section, please note any issues that apply in your life; each has a unique therapeutic demand.)

Biological and Genetic Issues

Those with predisposition represent the percentage of our population that has the inborn, genetic predisposition to developing a Monkey Brain. Patrick Carnes PhD, in his book on sex addiction, *Don't Call it Love*, describes the cultural aspect of predisposition: "Certain children are especially susceptible to the addiction process. These children live in our addiction-prone culture. They probably have parents who are addicted to one or more behaviors or substances … most often the children are abused, probably in several ways. These children are the vulnerable children.

"… They seek to feel better. They are not bad children, but rather children in pain who seek relief. They will use 'highs' to feel better—food, sex, TV—whatever numbs the pain—for most potential sex addicts, masturbation will be a key coping mechanism and source of comfort." (Carnes, 1992)

Being hardwired for a Monkey Brain has an inevitable ring to it. Predisposition is a tendency, not a sentence. Those with predisposition who learn healthy emotional skills need not suffer an inevitable curse, but they do have a susceptibility that the others in the population do not have. It is an issue that "Normals" struggle to understand. Normals might wonder why the addict doesn't just say no. To them it is a choice—without a

Monkey Brain it is easy to see. The reality is that predisposed individuals are dealing with some dynamics not felt or understood by Normals.

Ann was a 36-year-old mother who was struggling with a serious meth addiction. She had dabbled in several drugs and used alcohol all of her life, but it was always on a take-it-or-leave-it basis. She used frequently, but could always walk away, and she never lost control or fell into excess. She was judgmental of some of her friends who had serious drug problems in her earlier years.

Then she met Tommy. Tommy mainlined meth, which at the time was a fairly new drug craze. With her open approach to drug use, Ann accepted Tommy's invitation to shoot up with him. Ann's description of what happened next really tells the story. "I fell in love! I used daily for the next three weeks until I crashed [in exhaustion]. When I woke up four days later, I couldn't wait to get a needle and go again."

Ann found a drug that triggered her predisposition, a high that was compelling beyond anything she had felt before. That is the problem for people of predisposition, sometimes the bus leaves the station without warning.

Here is another example:

Millie really didn't have a drug or alcohol problem until she was in her mid-thirties. Millie was raised in a family with a significant alcohol and drug abuse history. Millie, however, had managed to dodge the addiction bullet. She had always been successful in her work, was college-educated, and enjoyed many friends. When her husband of 12 years left her and their son very unexpectedly, she was devastated. She began to drink for comfort; and in a very short time, was drinking for the sake of drinking.

What had held no interest for her earlier in her life now became Millie's demon. Her predisposition came into play when it was combined with the devastation she felt from the sudden abandonment by her husband.

Childhood Trauma

Survivors of childhood physical, emotional or sexual abuse—as well as victims of traumatic events—and the abandoned children (by parents either absent emotionally or not present physically) often resort to medicating on the way to becoming addicted. They find comfort from the emotional pain in their lives. It begins as a coping strategy, which through the conditioning process becomes compulsion and addiction.

There is something missing in their emotional development. Their emotional foundation was never completed and they struggle to function. We have great difficulty meeting our needs without that foundation. Maslow suggested the foundation was built of knowing that we would survive the day and that we were safe in the world. These children never had the comfort of knowing they were safe. Without establishing it, our other needs become very, very difficult to meet and our emotional dysfunction gets in the way.

This is a simplified version of Maslow's view of the order of our basic human needs (often referred to as Maslow's Hierarchy):

Survival—Having food and shelter to survive
Safety—Freedom from danger, safe and secure in the world
Loving and Being Loved
Accomplishment—Contributing in a meaningful way
Being the Best We Can Be (Maslow, 1962)

When, for example, safety is compromised by sexual abuse or trauma, the ability to meet the need to love and be loved (and all other needs below it on the list), are compromised. We struggle to love and be loved because we might suffer terrible jealousy or be so controlling (trying to be safe) that no one can stand to live with us. The emotional pain generated by such experience begs to be soothed. The self-nurturing relief of addiction seems to be the perfect solution in the beginning.

Tommy suffered from abandonment issues as a result of his drug-addicted mother. She was physically present, but unable to care for him or be available for him emotionally when she was lost in her addiction.

Tommy's aunt told him of a time when he was two, when she observed him dressed only in a messy diaper, crying and reaching up to his mother for her care and comfort. His mother pushed him aside because she was busy using and getting ready to shoot up with heroin. It was a symbolic moment of his childhood.

Tommy is now 21 and very interested in having a girlfriend, but he reports that his relationships never last more than a month or two. Andy is a heavy pot smoker. He is also decent looking and has a great sense of humor. He also has some very dysfunctional relationship behaviors.

He really wants to feel loved, but he comes off as very controlling. (He is still worrying about the possibility of more abandonment.) He feels a strong need to know everyone that his girlfriend has contact with. If they go to a party, Tommy cannot allow his girlfriend to be in a separate room because he is afraid she might meet and leave with someone else. After a few weeks, even though Tommy has a lot going for him, his girlfriends break off the relationship because they feel smothered by him.

Tommy turns to his bong for comfort, but it is never enough. In reality there is not enough marijuana on the planet to provide the comfort he needs.

Tommy is desperately trying to love and be loved, but he has never been able to establish that it is safe in this world or that he is loved and wanted. No one was ever there to confirm that for him.

Without establishing safety, he struggles at meeting his need to love and be loved. Now his addiction and neediness (his fear of further loss) get in the way, the controlling behavior drives away any potential girl-friends. The addiction certainly isn't meeting his needs either, although he thinks he feels better when he is high. Hence, the sentence for practicing dysfunctional ways is that we are forever trying to meet our needs in ways that can never meet our needs.

George: *Early in my therapy, my counselor said that I was the victim of trauma as a child. I argued this point vigorously saying that I always had my needs met; I had clothes, food, shelter, and was never beaten or hit as a child.*

What my counselor told me was that I was not subjected to physical trauma, but my family were experts in emotional trauma.

Some examples of my mother's favorite expressions come to mind:

"If you do this for me, I will love you more."

"I can never forgive you for what you did."

"Good children are seen and not heard, and better children are not seen."

"Wait until your father gets home; he'll talk some sense into you. And if he can't, he'll beat into you."

"You're the big one; your brother's the bright one."

My mother was the oldest of three, born when her parents were 16 years old. Her mother had a nervous breakdown shortly after my mother was born, so her parents gave her up to be raised by her grandmother, who lived close by.

Even after her brother and sister were born, my mother was never let back in the house and lived with her grandmother until she moved out to get married when she was 18 years old.

She was great at attaching strings to everything and shaming you to get what she wanted. If you wanted her accolades or acceptance, you were going to pay somehow. Love was something you earned, and forgiveness was not forthcoming, no matter what you did. If you did not deliver, you were shamed so badly that you would never come up short again.

My father was the youngest of three boys—a surprise with 13 years between him and middle son. He was of small stature. He moved out of the house at age 14 since his father had died years before and his mother hated him (for being a surprise). He lived in a boys' home until he met and married my mom at 18. Shortly after their marriage, he went off to World War II. By the time he came back for home leave he was a father, my older brother having been born while he was at war.

My father was absentee most of the time but was a strict authoritarian when he was around. He compensated for his perceived shortcomings by using his intellect as a weapon. No one questioned his decisions, and to question him or talk back to him was a request to be banished to the basement or your room. He liked to challenge you to arguments for the sole purpose of belittling or demeaning you. I heard the expression "In the battle of wits, you're unarmed" more times than I care to remember.

I know that neither of my parents had nurturing childhoods and accordingly could not provide one for my brother or me. They were doing the best they could when raising their own family. It took me 20 years of intense therapy to be able to say that sentence.

I learned "normal behavior" from these people. Is it any surprise that by the time I reached adulthood I was dysfunctional? My view of what was right/wrong, good/bad, healthy/unhealthy was so skewed I was almost doomed to become an addict. Certainly without counseling, which was just not done when I was growing up, there was little chance of a good outcome.

All of this trauma gets stored in the body if it isn't dealt with and comes back up at times when you least expect it. Many therapists espouse doing family of origin work and I share that belief. It can be incredibly powerful. The old expression comes to mind: those that do not learn from the past are destined to repeat it.

Shame-Based Personalities

What is shame? Shame is the disowning of one's personhood. It demands a cover-up so the disowned part can hide for protection in secrecy and darkness. Shame can also be seen as intense self-hatred, the ultimate product of parental or self-abuse and neglect. We learn to be ashamed of, and separate from, parts of us we judge to be rejectable when we are humiliated, ridiculed, or violated as children. We also can build a shame persona by focusing on our perceived failures and not learning the art of self-forgiveness. Shame has been called "the mother of all emotions" because it is used to conceal all the rest.

Shame and guilt can be contrasted in their message to the person. Guilt says, "I made a mistake," while shame delivers the message, "I am a mistake." When we experience the feeling of guilt, we blame our behavior, saying to ourselves, "How could I have done that? What can I do to make amends for what I have done?"

Shame, on the other hand, says, "What a stupid fool I am! I am worthless and no one will ever like me." In a healthy upbringing, parents teach children that shame and guilt are not the same. To the extent the early environment was unhealthy, the two feelings of shame and guilt are knit together.

"All emotions have specific uses and propel us toward action. Shame is linked to the need for protecting the vulnerable child. In a young person suffering parental abuse, there can be no safety outside himself, because he is dependent on others, who are victimizing caregivers, for his very life. Therefore, since rejection of the parents is not an option, the abused or neglected child internalizes that the problem must be me. There is something terribly wrong with me." (Smoky Rain Counseling Services)

And, oh my, the thinking errors shame can create. The harvest of shame is very painful. Self-hatred and loathing, self-resentment and anger, disappointment and mourning are but a few of the raw emotions harvested. Many turn to self-medicating to find relief.

Ruth calls what she is avoiding through her sexual addiction as "the sadness." It presents in her as a very profound sense of rejection, disappointment and shame. She states, "I just feel like I am not who I should be."

She first became aware of the feeling after singing a song at her first-grade holiday concert. As she returned to her seat, feeling very proud and hoping she had pleased her parents, her father asked, "Why didn't you smile?" The comment cut through her to the core. She hadn't done it right; she didn't act the way she was supposed to, even though she had tried very, very hard.

As an attractive, bright 36-year-old, she still bore the sadness and shame and only found relief in the euphoria associated with falling in love. Relationship after relationship would mask the pain, but not heal it. She went from partner to partner, in a constant state of falling in love, but never quieting the sadness or feeling worthy.

When Ruth began to heal her shame and realized she was exactly who she was supposed to be, she didn't need "medication" anymore, and the need to engage in her addiction diminished. Real changes started happening in her life. Addictive behaviors have less hold on us when underlying issues are resolved.

Early Sexualization

Children exposed to sexual content before maturation are susceptible to the lure of sexual addictions.

Peter was raised by what he describes as "hippie" parents. He has vivid memories of drug and alcohol use from an early age. He was allowed to begin using marijuana and LSD at age five. His parents and friends often had sex in areas where he could observe them, and he began reenacting the sexual activities he had witnessed with his younger sister when he was 10.

At age 41, he came to my office, struggling to kick what he described as a nasty alcohol addiction. He could consume legendary amounts of alcohol and maintain a semblance of function. He was surprised to find out that having had upwards of 65 sexual partners might mean he also had a sexual addiction.

Early sexualization is, by nature of our sexually explicit culture, increasingly affecting our children. It is like trying to run a 110-volt appliance with 220-volt current. The wiring is just too delicate to handle the tremendous voltage. Young developing minds are likewise incapable of handling the highly charged sexually explicit material that seems available at every turn.

Recreational User That Got Off the Trail

These are experimenters and recreational users that fall prey to their own conditioning behaviors. These are like Pinocchio when he went to the fair and realized at the end of the day, much to his surprise, that he wasn't a little boy.

If we think of addiction in a linear way, beginning with recreational or experimental use that progresses to compulsive use and then to addictive use, we can begin to understand these addicts. It is really about conditioning. The forming of a bond between difficult emotions and a drug of choice. The same process Pavlov demonstrated with his now-famous dogs. Pavlov noticed his dogs' salivated when he brought them food. One day he began to ring a bell when he brought the food. After a time, he noted that if only the bell rang, it caused the dogs to salivate whether or not food was present.

They had become "conditioned" to react in a particular way. The dogs had grown to associate getting fed with hearing a bell. Recreational users are, without being aware, conditioning themselves. Each time they use, the emotional center makes note: "I don't feel my anxiety (or any other difficult emotion) when I drink." With continued use, that realization grows into a strong emotional bond between our stressors and the need for our drug of choice.

In the beginning, it might just be an occasional weekend social event, but as the connection is made—and reinforced—that relief from difficult feelings comes from our drug of choice, we make steady progress towards compulsion and addiction. When the emotional bond has been formed, the individual no longer waits for a social event to drink because it has become about more than being social. The emotional center sends out a request for consumption whenever difficult feelings arise.

Soon a compulsive feature to the conditioning develops. With compulsion, the individual's urge to drink is greater that his will to say no and the addictive process really takes off. Eventually full-blown addiction sets in, where the individual is drinking for no other reason than he needs alcohol to function. That first drink in the morning steadies his hands and removes the pain from his body. It is not recreational or experimental any longer. It is dependence … full-blown addiction.

Spiritual Replacement

There is an inherent loneliness about life on earth. Some feel it more acutely than others. For an individual who has had little or no spiritual upbringing or influence, the comfort of indulgence, in the beginning, eases the pain of not having spiritual connection. It fills a spiritual void. One alcoholic said of it, "I have been looking for something all my life. I don't yet know what it is … I will know it when I find it." She thought for many years it was in the bottle. She now knows it is not. She is still looking.

Scott Peck has offered that "addiction is a disease of the soul … the ultimate loneliness." (Peck, 1993) Our addiction does separate us from our Higher Power. Because of the progressive nature of the disease, the separation increases as we stay in our addiction. Our new god is a very jealous god and is not interested in sharing us with anyone. We increase our isolation, become more devoted to our compulsions, and lose ourselves more completely with each passing addictive day.

As we ponder our addiction's genealogy, it is worth noting that some of us have several of these elements present. There is not a single solitary underlying cause. For the addict, finding the underlying issue(s) helps "make sense" of his addiction and helps in the process of restoring hope. For the clinician it gives direction to treatment.

Recovery in this area is two-pronged. The addict should work to resolve underlying issues, thereby diminishing their emotional stranglehold. At the same time, the addict should develop new emotional management skills that increase both his tolerance and his ability to deal with emotional discomfort. Bringing down the emotional effect of underlying issues and raising the ability to tolerate emotional challenges can bring the two into healthy manageable balance.

And Besides All That,
Our Culture Doesn't Help Either

Men Don't Cry!

George: *My single most traumatic and scarring experience was with my father around this very topic. I was 11 years old and my father told me that the family dog had been hit by a car and killed. When I heard the news, I was very upset and sat down on the steps and started to cry. My father's reaction was to open hand slap me across the face and say those magic words, "Men don't cry; be a man; stop crying."*

I can remember it like it was a few moments ago. I could feel the anger and rage build up as I rubbed my cheek where he'd slapped me. I remember thinking, "You son of a bitch, I don't know how, or when, but you will pay for that."

Our relationship was never the same after that day. I developed such anger and rage that it tainted every interaction I had with him. We became distant and I did whatever I could to get even with him or avoid him completely. It wasn't until 30 years later that I came to terms with my rage and resentment toward him.

It was no surprise to me when I later learned that there had not been a car accident at all; my father had taken the dog to the vet and had him put down. Instead of owning up to reality, he made up a story so I would not be upset with him, which is what happened anyway.

It was the era for men not showing emotions, after World War II and Korea post-traumatic stress wasn't even thought of. You could get diagnosed with shell shock, but beyond that you were supposed to man up, not show your emotions, not talk about being scared or afraid, and just get on with your life. Any wonder there are so many issues in today's society?

Asking for Help Is a Sign of Weakness

George: *This was another family lesson. My father and mother both would criticize me if I could not solve a problem on my own. Worse still was when I asked for help and had trouble "getting it." My father could not abide that at all.*

I recall having trouble with algebra in high school and asking my father for help. You know the kind of question: "Let X equal the speed of the train leaving station A." Why is that X? What do I do with that? Who cares about the train anyway? Where's the training going? What time did it leave?

He got so frustrated trying to teach me that he gave up and asked one of his friends to come over and help me. "Maybe you can teach my idiot son," he told him. His friend did help me and I wound up getting an A on the statewide exam in algebra (and won placement the following year in an advanced math class). Regardless of my accomplishments, my father thought of me as stupid after that and would never offer help.

I learned not to ask for fear of eliciting his anger. When I questioned my mother about it, she just said "You know how you father is; don't bother him unless it is something really important."

A Real Man Gets a Lot of Women!

George: *How does society measure a man? By his good works, generosity, financial success, kindness? Or, do you think Saint Peter at the Pearly Gates asks, "How many women did you have sex with?" And he only admits those with the highest count. While I can't say for certain, having never been there, I suspect that is not on his list of questions to ask.*

I have a sponsee who measures his success in life by the number of sex partners one has. He includes in this count the women he has paid to have sex with him and wears it like a badge of honor. He thinks this is perfectly okay and is a good measure of him as a man. He is fixated on the concept of an alpha male being someone who goes around with a constant erection having sex with anything with a pulse and the guy who has had the most women at the end wins.

He desperately wants to be an alpha male, so much so that he has taken classes and bought books on subjects like how to pick up women and convince them to have sex with you.

He has been a tough one to help in recovery with this paradigm. No wonder he suffers from the compulsive behavior of sex with prostitutes. If one is good, two is better, four is better still, and so on and so on. I asked him why multiple partners are so important to him. He said, "It just is; it is the real mark of a man."

I said, "Really, can you prove that?"

He confessed that most men who behaved like that were frequently a societal pariah, but he still admired anyone who had sex with a lot of women.

So I asked, "Why?"

Folks, "just because" is not an answer to that question. To make my point, I brought up his recent efforts to get into graduate school. I asked him, "Is that question on the application, how many women you've had sex with?"

He said, "No."

I followed up by asking, "Have you ever been asked that question by anyone, how many women you've had sex with?"

Again, he said, "No."

So I asked him my favorite question in conclusion. "Do you think there is a reason for that? What can we learn from this?"

He is in the early stages of dealing with this faulty thinking. He suffers from feeling one-down. As a child, he was picked on by his parents, older brother, and friends. He immigrated to the US and got picked on by his classmates for being a minority.

As a result, he had a desperate need to show his worth, that he was better-than and not less-than. What better way to compensate for this than having sex with multiple partners. He would show the world what a man he is and boast about it if the subject ever came up.

It is interesting to me to note that he picked me as a sponsor because he thought I was a real alpha male. In his mind I didn't care what other people thought of me because of the shoes I frequently wear (checkered sneakers). To him my shoes said I don't care what other people think of me.

I can report that I am definitely not an alpha male and what other people might think of me never crossed my mind when picking out those shoes. I liked them because they were comfortable and cheap and I didn't have to bend over to tie them.

Chapter 3

There Is Another Way
Finding It Is Recovery

SECTION I: PREPARATION

Reclaiming the addicted brain is recovery. It only happens when our Monkey Brain gets turned off. Finding the "off" switch to the Monkey Brain while using the Monkey Brain is problematic. Like everything else, it doesn't want to die. The Monkey Brain doesn't want to give up control and will do anything to survive intact. Learning how to outmaneuver the Monkey Brain in the early stages of recovery is the purpose of this chapter. This is the "How To" of "Reclaiming Your Addicted Brain."

Some believe that "hitting bottom" is required and is the most effective "off" switch for the Monkey Brain since it leads to the realization that something needs to change; however, the collateral damage can be horrific. Hitting bottom often entails losing one's family, job, house, life savings, or even one's life. Wouldn't it be better if the bottom could be "raised" by confronting thinking errors, participating in honesty and accountability, and developing the recovery skills of a reclaimed brain. Better if we can wake up, come to ourselves, make changes, and retire our Monkey Brain before we lose everything.

The good news—born out in research—is that our brains are very resilient, "plastic" being the clinical term. That means the brain is able to change (i.e., rewire the way it thinks) based on experiences. The challenge is to find the right collection of experiences (behaviors, thoughts, and actions) that encourage the demise of Monkey Brain, and apply consistent, sustained effort in practicing them.

Some describe it as building new neural pathways in the brain. Neural pathways connect areas of the brain and the nervous system with actions and behaviors. These are the pathway habits used in the brain, they are the "autopilot" mode, seemingly more reflexive than the result of conscious thoughts.

Addiction builds neural pathways that have a super-highway quality. Once we hit the "on ramp" of an addiction pathway, we end up acting out, a process that is both quick and certain. Even when recognized in advance, the outcome seems inevitable, like watching a car skidding downhill on ice until it hits something. No matter what the driver does, the car is going to slide down the hill. Building new pathways that take a new course and result in a different outcome is the goal.

Alta Mira Recovery sums up neuroplasticity this way:

New thoughts and skills carve out new pathways.

Repetition and practice strengthen these pathways, forming new habits.

Old pathways get used less and weaken.

With repeated and direct attention toward a desired change, we all have the ability to rewire our brains.

Develop a Recovery Work Ethic

With repeated and direct attention, many examples presented throughout our story illustrate the need for a healthy recovery work ethic. Half-measures avail us nothing, and those who have found freedom and serenity will testify that three-quarter or seven-eighth measures render no results. Whatever it takes! has to be the attitude.

There is a reason for the term "WORK of Recovery." It should be self-evident that results only come when we put in the work. Reversing the conditioning process of our addiction and creating new neural pathways takes consistent, sustained work.

Pavlov unconditioned his dogs by not bringing food at the ringing of the bell. If we are consistent in not bringing our acting out into play when our addiction bell rings (what many would call our triggers), we make progress. When we are inconsistent in our effort and allow episodes of acting out, our addiction is strengthened rather than weakened and new neural pathways always seem under construction but never are completed.

The Nanticoke Indian Tribe holds this legend: One evening, an elderly Cherokee brave told his grandson about a battle that goes on inside people.

He said, "My son, the battle is between two wolves inside us all. One is evil. It is anger, envy, jealousy, sorrow, regret, greed, arrogance, self-pity, guilt, resentment, inferiority, lies, false pride, superiority, and ego.

"The other is good. It is joy, peace, love, hope, serenity, humility, kindness, benevolence, empathy, generosity, truth, compassion, and faith."

"Which wolf wins?" asked the grandson.

The old Cherokee simply replied, "The one that you feed."

(*Hint:* A serious recovery work ethic feeds the good wolf.)

As one recovery quote puts it, "You don't get over an addiction by stopping using. You recover by creating a new life where it is easier to not use. If you don't create a new life, then all the factors that brought you to your addiction will catch up with you again."

Newcomers to Alcoholics Anonymous (AA) are often introduced to the "90 meetings in 90 days" concept. Immersing oneself in the work is the pathway to a happy ending. One of the complications of recovery work is that the battle is fought on many fronts; like the juggler keeping six balls in the air, there is a lot to attend to. New behaviors must be learned, new skills gained concurrently, old strong urges must be ignored and retired. There is a body of work required to achieve recovery. It demands consistent, persistent, enlightened effort and complete engagement.

Do some work every day for your recovery. Reading, meditating, calling a recovery buddy, accountability buddy or others in the struggle, attending a meeting, therapy or an appointment with a sponsor should all have a regular place in the recovering addict's schedule. These activities create the "aha" moments of healing and progress. These growth moments will escape us if we do not do the work.

Be on the lookout for your addict voice here. The Monkey Brain recognizes the danger for himself if you actually do the work of recovery. Excuses will crop up like weeds in a garden. "I'm too tired for the meeting tonight." "I can never get hold of my sponsor." "Meditating puts me to sleep." "Meetings are boring with the same people sharing the same old stories week after week." All are Monkey Brain efforts at survival. Use your best disputations and move on to doing what you should be doing. Establish a good recovery work ethic and preserve it with commitment.

George: *Change is a very scary thing for me. I know the most challenging changes in life are getting married, getting divorced, moving, or losing a loved one. Although not mentioned, admitting I had an addiction and that I needed help is right up there. Taking action, i.e., getting help, is difficult, too.*

I know I am a creature of habit and, what is more, I do not like to deal with uncertainty. I used to ride the train into New York City to work and it was amusing to see people get on the same train and sit in the same seat every day—and how anxious they became if someone was in their seat. It could set them off for the whole day.

Of course, I did exactly the same thing and could be quite incensed if someone was in MY seat. The nerve. Didn't they know this seat belonged to me, and how dare they sit in it! The point is that we all like routine and feel uncomfortable when something changes the status quo. When something does upset us, we either suffer from inertia or denial. When this happens, we feel a need to make these unpleasant feelings go away, so we medicate.

Early in therapy, when trying to establish new thought processes, my therapist asked me to think of how I act and how many rituals I have established that give me comfort, like when and how I make the bed, brush my teeth, get dressed, drive to/from work, where I eat lunch. All of these routines give me comfort and make me feel safe. Changing these routines requires conscious effort and thought.

When warning signs crop up we often ignore them, dismiss them as an odd-ity or an aberration that is not worthy of attention. I remember one morning my hand was shaking and thinking, "Gee, that is odd, that has never happened before." I never thought to connect that to the fact that I had been binge drinking for the previous ten days. How could they be related? Must be something else.

If you're fan of one of the sitcoms on TV, you have seen one character drive her car even though the check engine light is on, and she continues driving it right up until the car dies and she has to buy a new one. Inertia or denial? Either way, she was stopped dead in her tracks (She hit bottom). Of course, addressing new issues causes discomfort, a dis-ease.

Getting Ready to Reclaim the Brain

The process of building new neural pathways that will lead to reclaiming your addicted brain occurs on a continuum, and those afflicted with Monkey Brainitis can only absorb and accept messages that are appropriate for their particular position on the continuum.

An example would be discussing treatment options with a client who has no interest or intention of quitting. The client is not interested in that conversation—and quite resistant to having it. The clinician might present, argue, discuss, implore, but the client will be having none of it. The Monkey Brain will not allow it.

Monkey Brain's domination must be interrupted and the addict allowed to move along the change continuum to where he might entertain the notion that treatment may be needed. That movement will enable the client to participate in a conversation about treatment options. Movement may take time, much more than most want, and always requires consistent, sustained effort.

New neural pathways are constructed as the client moves through the stages, each stage contributing to the construction process. Helpers and clients that can recognize the current stage can expedite the process dramatically. If the client can be met where he is, in whatever stage that might be, and clinically helped to the next stage, and then the next, recovery can occur and the Monkey Brain be rewired and retired. The client's current stage of change reveals the next recovery need.

An addict who has no interest in even thinking about changing would be said to be in "pre-contemplation stage" of change. This is the normal "setting" of the Monkey Brain. His voice sounds like this: "My life is fine. There are no problems with my substance use or anything else I'm doing." The addict isn't in much danger of healing or changing in this stage.

He might move to the "contemplation stage" when consequences build up to the undeniable level, but he is not really entertaining any ideas about how change would occur. This is the "edge of the world" for the Monkey Brain, and without intervention or the hitting of rock bottom, it is the normal turning-back point of any positive change thoughts. It is a step the Monkey Brain struggles to take. This is a "bridge too far" for the Monkey Brain.

In contemplation, the addict asks himself if he should stop using. In moments of clarity, the addict starts thinking about what change might be like or how it might occur, thereby entering the "preparation stage."

As the client learns skills to diminish the dependence on the Monkey Brain, he may be ready to enter the "action stage," where changes are made. "Maintenance" is the last stage of change. It is the process of keeping the changes in place and leaving Monkey Brain thinking behind. (Tomlin 2004)

Movement through the stages of change occurs as the result of gaining clarity through the work of recovery. Something resonates within from a reading, attending a meeting, therapeutic work, step work, or meetings with a sponsor, all can provide the clarity of "aha" moments. These are the realizations that allow us to see things in a new way. This is the process of building a new neural pathway.

We do not heal alone. The Monkey Brain resists that. We need to find clarity, seeing our reality without the Monkey Brain filter, and we need the assistance of others to accomplish that, especially early on in the recovery process.

Russell Crowe in the part of John Nash in the movie *A Beautiful Mind* shows us how. Nash, a Nobel Laureate in Economics, is beset with paranoid schizophrenia; he has a great deal of difficulty deciphering who and what are real. In one scene, he is engaged in a three-way conversation with a person known to be real to him and a stranger.

After a bit, he turns to the known friend and asks, "Is this person real?" With the affirmative response, the conversation continues. This is how Nash managed to function at a high level in spite of his disease.

In the beginning of our recovery work, we need to seek that type of input for our thoughts and behaviors. We need the help of discerning information not created by our Monkey Brain in our decision-making. Most find this in recovery meetings, sponsors, therapists, recovery friends, self-help books, and the like.

Without help, the Monkey Brain oscillates between pre-contemplation and contemplation, in no danger of changing anything. Addicts are lost in their addictions until the harsh realities of hitting a bottom and its attendant suffering bring them to action. The alternative? Fully embracing their suffering and self-destruction, becoming lost forever to their demon.

George: *My addiction was like any other ritual. I used it to medicate to feel better. Although it can be quite risky, I felt at ease during the process as it was known and got the desired results.*

Changing this behavior was challenging. Of course, first I needed to recognize it (step 1), but then I needed to do something about it, i.e., change. Here is where a lot of emotions interfere and inertia sets in, mostly around the fear of change.

Change and its resulting uncertainty were a scary thing for me. I would either avoid it or make up great excuses why I should not make a change. The "what if" abyss. I went from uniformed optimism thinking about the change to informed pessimism as I worked my way through it.

Recently I had to move my mother-in-law to an assisted-living facility. She is 88 and it was time. She was no longer showering, wearing clean clothes, taking her medications properly, etc.

Actually, it was more than time. All of her children ignored the telltale signs of her losing her ability to function on her own. Instead, they observed her quirks (wearing the same clothes every day) and rationalized how despite them she was doing so well for her age (inertia). There were no outward signs of her being in trouble, so, let's not upset her and leave her where she is. Of course, if you asked her if she wanted to move the answer was short and concise, "No!"

So we waited and waited until she was really suffering. When we finally moved her, it almost killed her. She was so disoriented by all the changes that she withdrew, stopped eating and socializing, and became very angry and impossible to deal with.

Despite all the good intention, we did the worst thing we could have done. Think about it. Do you move someone while they're well and healthy and can endure the changes? Or do you wait until they're frail and dependent and any change throws them into turmoil. If we had acted in a more timely manner, the resulting upset would have been less severe.

I had a similar situation with my drinking. I thought I hid it so well, but I was the only one who thought that way. A few years after I stopped drinking, I was talking to one of my friends and asked him if he ever thought I had a drinking problem.

He said, "Oh God, yes; we knew you were in trouble but didn't want to say anything. We thought you were out of control."

As it turned out, I was out of control. I suppose they needed me to be in an accident, arrested for drunk driving, or hospitalized before they would intervene. Don't wait to see what happens. If you're an addict, what happens next will be worse than what is happening now.

You can take that to the bank.

One Man's Journey

I decided on one mission in life, "To make the world a better place." Sounds like a huge task, but, how do I do that? I know if I don't drink and I don't act out sexually, the world is a better place. Mission accomplished!

George: *The hardest question for me to answer is, "What finally changed in me such that I actually started to recover?" What made the difference? How did I stop spinning my wheels and gain traction? Why did what I tried before suddenly start working when it didn't work before?*

I thought and thought about this and pondered my life in search of the silver bullet that helped me get sober. The more I thought, the more I realized it was not one thing—there was no silver bullet. Instead it was a perfect storm of several things that made the difference.

I received the gift of desperation. I finally realized that half measures and my best thinking were not going to get me sober. I was humbling to admit defeat but it had to happen.

Next, I need a dynamic recovery plan. Something to work on all fronts at the same time.

I call it a recovery stool that has four legs. Each leg is essential to my recovery. No shortcuts, no picking and choosing what you want to work, no half-measures. I had to get all four things right or it wasn't going to work. The legs of the stool are:

- *Living the first three steps of the recovery program*
- *Getting the right therapist and being honest with him and doing everything you're told*
- *Getting the right sponsor and doing everything you're told*
- *Getting the right pharmaceutical assistance*

LEG ONE: *Live the first three steps of the recovery program*

George: *You will note that I did not say thinking that way—I really mean living that way. I had read the first three steps hundreds of times, but even then I still thought I could control my acting out.*

In an AA meeting I heard a member say, "I don't have a drinking problem I have a thinking problem." That made me realize that was exactly what I had—a thinking problem. I was trying to lead my recovery instead of letting my recovery lead me. I thought I was pretty smart, certainly smarter than the 12 Steps, and definitely smarter than all the other folks I dealt with, including my sponsor and therapist. Well, I was wrong, I couldn't have been more wrong. Once I decided I'd had enough and was willing to do anything it took to get sober, I actually started to recover.

Amazing, isn't it?

Many of us have heard AA's Step 3: "Made a decision to turn our will and lives over to the care of our Higher Power as we understood him." Often it's translated into the shorthand of "live life on life's terms."

The Big Book of AA says much on this subject, which will not be repeated here. Certainly addicts like me love to be the playwright, casting agent, producer, and director of their lives. They try to manipulate reality by lying or telling half-truths. (Only an addict can draw a distinction between the two.) Usually with disastrous results.

What does this mean to you? Do you sit around and stare at the sky waiting for a message from God? Do you go to church on Sunday and ask the Reverend if he needs anything done, like washing the floors, cleaning the bathrooms, taking out the garbage? Do you dedicate your life to helping the poor or downtrodden? Or do you determine God's will another way?

Some break this step down and say all you need to do is make a decision to turn your life and will over—that you don't need to do anything more than that. In my opinion, there is much more to it than that.

One tool that works well is to consider your life a series of lessons. With each lesson there is an opportunity to demonstrate what you have learned. Either by making a good decision (do the next right thing) or a bad decision (do the next wrong thing). If you get it right, another situation will present itself and you get to make yet another decision. If you get it wrong, soon enough another situation will present itself and you get to make yet another decision. It goes on forever.

A simple example of this principle: You sit down to eat lunch in your favorite restaurant. You look at the menu and think, "I could have a chef's salad, but the bacon cheeseburger looks awfully good. I think I'll have that." Not that we have anything against cheeseburgers, but one of these choices is better for your body than the other. Likewise, what do you want to have to drink? Do you have a beer, wine, iced tea, or plain water? Each decision has its own implications.

Since we are all human beings and by definition are perfectly imperfect, we won't make the right decision all the time—nor are we expected to. However, the addict has a pretty bad average for making good decisions. Usually due to their faulty thinking and disconnect from reality. Regardless of your track record, if you try to do the next right thing, your average will improve.

Another way to think of this is by using an analogy of a professional baseball player. The player gets up to bat with the full intention of hitting the ball, hard and probably out of the park. He has practiced hitting, gone through rigorous physical training, and has the mental image of what it is like to hit the ball. Does he hit it out of the park every time? No. Does he even hit it every time? Of course not. But his intent is the same every time. He doesn't think to make only half an effort. He isn't distracted by other things in his life. He is focused on hitting the ball. An addict needs to approach making life decisions the same way.

When addicts are feeling sorry for themselves, one-down, depressed, hungry, angry, lonely, tired, or otherwise less-than, it is hard for them to remember the original intent or to approach any decision with their full attention. Too many times they give in to temptation, the desire to medicate, and say, "I deserve this." Which exacerbates their original bad feelings.

After two years of trying, I realized that half-measures weren't working for me. I was in the program, doing what was expected, or as much as I deemed appropriate anyway. However, I wasn't getting any better and was still in terrible pain. I had the outward signs of recovery. Inside I was still sick and very much in denial.

Admitting to myself that what I was doing wasn't working was the hardest thing I've done.

On my first foray working the steps, I had this brilliant idea. Go straight to Step 9 and make amends. I thought that was perfectly sane. The fact that I hadn't done any of the work before that was a mere technicality at best, nuisance at worst.

I knew I was out of control, I was sorry for what I had done and I wanted to make amends for it. What better way to tell everyone I was in recovery and getting better than to make amends! Besides, the real win-win was that I could legitimately (in my mind anyway) contact all my acting-out partners and tell them how sorry I was for what I had done (and it just so happens, see how they were doing). I didn't have to do any of that other work. Clearly some of the steps were a good idea and others, well, not so much. Here is a recap of my take on each step:

Step 1. I certainly believed in Step 1; I knew I was unmanageable. Any idiot could see that. But that didn't mean I had to actually do anything. Of course, once having agreed with that, I immediately proceeded to try to manage things on my own. You can imagine who well that worked.

Steps 2 & 3. Spirituality was a complete anathema to me. I heard the 12 Steps were a spiritual program but figured that was a nice to have, not a "have to have." Besides I didn't really need spirituality. I had abandoned religion in my youth and felt no need to go back to it now. I worked in an engineering/science-dominated field and there was no room for God there.

To me, "higher power" was shorthand for God, and I felt he had turned his back on me years ago. If he didn't need me, I didn't need him. Besides wasn't he man's fabrication anyway, like the tooth fairy, the Easter bunny and Santa Claus. I could do things on willpower. I'd lived my entire life that way up to this point, so why change now.

Step 4. I knew what was wrong with me. I didn't need to make a list. Besides, someone might find it and then I would be in trouble. What if my wife found it? That would be a bad thing. Nope, no records or audit trail.

Steps 5 through 8. *These four steps were all bureaucracy. I was working with a sponsor and he knew what was going on. He had heard my story and knew what was wrong with me. So that was done. I had been asking God to remove my defects of character for years for all the good that did me, so just check these steps off as done.*

Step 9. *Amends … that was the key. They would free me. I liked them. It made sense to me. So, I said, "Let's get straight to the heart of the matter and make amends." And as I mentioned before, this had the added benefit that I could legitimately contact all my old acting-out partners and show them how much better I was.*

Steps 10 through 12. *This was just more spirituality baloney, so I figured I could get there when I get there.*

I don't think I need to tell you how much of a disaster this approach was. Let's put it this way: I went straight from the starting gate directly into the ditch. I did not pass go and did not collect $200. Unfortunately for me, I was stuck in this ditch for two more years.

My therapist told me to stare at myself in the mirror and take account of what I saw. I did that and did not like what I saw one bit. I was going through the motions; my heart wasn't in it. Sure I wanted the pain to go away, but I was unwilling to follow instructions or do any real work.

Like being in grade school and doing just enough to get by and keep my parents off my back. B's were fine, A's were too hard. My sponsor and my therapist actually wanted me to work. So for the first two years I accepted B's or maybe C's and I was good with that.

My recovery work included going to meetings, seeing a therapist, working with a sponsor, and working the steps. I did this because that is what I was told to do. I was going through the motions, believing that was enough—but not believing that I was sick or that I had any real work to do. I put my recovery as number one, but I was not putting my all into it and certainly not living my life that way.

I am a people pleaser; I do whatever it takes to make other people happy— whether I believe in it or not. Just so they will leave me alone. My wife wanted me to see a therapist. My therapist wanted me to have a sponsor. My sponsor wanted me to go to meetings and work the steps. All I wanted was to do the least possible and have the pain stop—and for all these people to stop bothering me. So I did those things, but with my head and not my heart, hoping I could do just enough and get by.

I went to meetings without ever saying a word. I never spoke to a soul. Except for the introductions part, I bet no one even knew my name. Not their fault, mine! I met with a therapist and told half-truths about what was going on (see section below). I met with my sponsor and did as little as I possibly could, never putting my heart into the work. I felt he understood addiction but did not understand me.

When I finally admitted my life was unmanageable, that no human power could relieve my addictive behavior, and that a Higher Power could and would if I sought a Higher Power, I made progress. Again, it is not a matter of thinking that way, it involves acting that way. I am a control freak, and evaluating and designing internal controls in a large corporation was my job, so I believed everything was in my control.

I was used to being the writer, director, casting agent, and producer. Living my life any other way just made no sense to me. Sure I could recite the first three steps but I didn't live like that. I kept trying to control every situation and have it turn out the way I wanted.

The idea of admitting I was powerless and acting that way was too much. Until it wasn't. Now I joke that I have turned my will and my life over to my Higher Power, but I still set my alarm clock. While I have given up control of the outcome, I still realize I have an active role in keeping my side of the street clean and must act accordingly.

One tool I use now is that when I feel too committed to a specific outcome, I back away and let things happen. This is true for my relationships with family and friends. I am honest and speak of my feelings and they make the decisions they deem appropriate. I do not try to manipulate them for my preferred outcome. I do, however, buy concert tickets and plane tickets in advance, and set the alarm. All of that is on my side of the street.

LEG TWO: *Get the right therapist;*
Be honest with him/her; and do everything you're told

George: *It is probably worth noting that I started therapy in 1990. I went to therapy weekly for 18 years religiously—and thought it was a joke. I likened my life to a bad Woody Allen movie: always in therapy, always suffering, never getting any better. It wasn't until 2008, when I went to an intensive program, that I was diagnosed as an alcoholic and a sex addict. How did I interact with the professionals I paid to help me for all those years?*

First, I thought I was smarter than they were, so I used the menu option of doing what they recommended.

Second, I told them only part of my story, but never the whole thing. I felt if I did, they would tell me to do something I wouldn't want to do.

Third, I didn't respect their advice since in most cases they themselves were divorced or had obvious emotional issues. I figured if they couldn't run their own lives, how on earth could they help me run mine.

So what do we learn from this. Lying or telling half-truths to your therapist gets you nowhere. Of course if you don't want to make any progress, this approach is just fine. When you do decide you're serious, a good therapist is an important resource and honesty with him/her is absolutely essential.

They are not mind readers; they can only respond to what you tell them. In a meeting with a close friend, he told me he had the same issue with his therapist. He had been a drug user for years and often went in to his weekly sessions either strung out or high as a kite. He could never understand why he was not diagnosed as an addict but never said to his therapist, "I think I have a problem with drugs."

My current and best therapist treats sessions like a business transaction. She says: "You're paying me $200 for this hour; what do you want out of it?" I liked that. Plan the work and work the plan. That got me to prioritize what was going wrong in my life at the moment and what I wanted as an outcome.

We set specific goals for each session and worked on specific action steps to address those goals as homework. The following sessions I had to report on what I did and whether it worked or didn't work. These sessions left me feeling hopeful and energized, excited to take the actions I need to take to get better.

Something I had not experienced with a therapist before.

In the old days, I would leave my sessions feeling lost, confused, angry and depleted. My therapists would ask, "What happened last week?" and then follow up with "and how does that make you feel?" The internal answer was always, "I feel like crap. How do you think I feel?" The outward answer was "I'm okay, but my wife did this or my boss said that and I am frustrated and angry that no one treats me the way I want to be treated."

Talking about your feelings can be cathartic; however, all it does is help you recognize and identify your feelings. It does not help you get in touch with the "why" and "what do I do about it?"

The other thing my current therapist has is a great bullshit meter. Whenever I go off track or start throwing bull around, she calls me on it and says: "That's a load of crap. You aren't being genuine with me. Don't tell me what you want me to hear or take the easy way out. Tell me the truth so we can deal with it." Boy, do I ever need someone who will talk to me like that.

Here's an example of how I used to act and how my addict mind worked its magic:

My early therapist(s) would ask me about my drinking (from 1990 to 2008).
Q. How many drinks did you have yesterday?
A. A couple.
Q. Can you be more specific?
A. Sure; two or three.
Q. Which is it, two or three?
A. Two. (My first and my last is what I really meant.)

I also had a very liberal idea of what constituted a drink. My drinks were four to six ounces of gin over a couple of ice cubes in an old-fashion glass. They never asked me how I defined a drink, and I never offered the information. The reality was that I would have five or six before dinner, then wine with dinner and then go back to gin afterwards.

So, in my mind that was two or three drinks (gin—wine—gin). I'm sure that if any of my therapists had that real information, they would have sent me to AA immediately. This went on for 18 years with no improvement in my condition.

At the same time I was also on antidepressants. I was told you can't take these with alcohol. So my addict brain said, "Don't take these with alcohol; take them with water and have a gin chaser." No flawed thinking there.

LEG THREE: *Get the right sponsor and do everything you're told*

George: *Finding the right sponsor and making a spiritual connection with him/her was essential in my recovery. The guidance—find someone who has what you want—is a good guideline, but it leaves a lot of room for error. Don't pick up the first person you ask and assume they will work for you. And if things don't work out, don't be afraid to find a new one. (However, don't be surprised if you have to start the steps all over again.)*

Of course, your sponsor is not your friend, or your higher power. He/she is a guide on how to work the steps. There is no set way to do this, and a sponsor is only a guide. I attend one weekly meeting with 70 participants, and I often ponder how many different recovery programs are at play. (My most conservative estimate is at least 70.)

The sponsor you choose should have the level of serenity, sobriety, and spirituality you want. Assess what they have and make sure there is a match-up to what you want. Although not essential, I do think it is beneficial to have a sponsor with a similar acting-out history so that you speak the same language.

I had repeated relationships outside my marriage. Working with a sponsor whose acting-out behavior was in homosexual relationships didn't work for me. It might for you, but it didn't for me.

I ultimately found someone of a similar professional background with almost the same addiction. Your sponsor is an important choice you need to think about. Don't just pick the first guy/gal who writes down that they are willing to sponsor. Interview them and see if you are a good fit. What is it about them that you are attracted to? Do you speak the same language emotionally and intellectually?

That is what I do whenever I take on a new sponsee: I treat it like an interview and see if this is someone who identifies with me and with whom I can identify. If it doesn't seem like a good fit, I tell them I think they should find someone else. No harm, no foul.

As I transitioned through the program and became a sponsor, I had the following experience. I am in my early 60s and retired, and this young man, in his early 20s, approached me to be his sponsor. We had similar acting-out behaviors—not exactly the same, but there was enough overlap and connection that we agreed to work together. In the first meetings we seemed to connect and have a good rapport.

After a few months, he mentioned that I had what he wanted. So I asked him specifically what he meant by that. His reply startled me. He said, "You have a great car, a nice house, and a Rolex watch—and I want all of those things."

I told him that that was not what is meant by the program. Material things are not what it's about. Spirituality and serenity are what you're looking for. Shortly thereafter, he dropped me as a sponsor because he was constantly relapsing. He found someone else, who had a nice car, house, and watch. My last check on him revealed that he has been in and out of rehab several times with no real recovery to speak of.

Another young man approached me after a meeting to be his sponsor. Per my process, we agreed to meet. In going through the interview, I asked him why he chose me to be his sponsor.

He said, "I like your shoes; I have the same pair. I figured any dude your age who had the nerve to wear shoes like that at your age would be a good sponsor for me." As it turned out, we were a good fit for other reasons than our taste in footwear and we worked extremely well together. The point is: suss out the situation and make sure you fit together. If things go well, this is a relationship that will last for a long time.

Once you find a sponsor, do what they tell you to do. Don't intellectualize or rationalize why one piece of advice is good or bad, just "do it" to borrow shamelessly from Nike's motto.

In a weekly session with one sponsee, I asked him how he was doing with his inner-circle behavior. In the two years I've worked with him, he has been unable to maintain more than 60 days sober. He made an interesting comment at our last meeting: "Every time I do what you tell me to do, things go well. And then I stop doing those things and I start to wobble and then I act out. I should really keep doing what you tell me to do."

He's frustrating to deal with because he understands what to do, but doesn't do it. He is trying to think himself sober and not act himself into sobriety. It is *not an intellectual program; you cannot think yourself sober. Action is required.*

Recently I heard that one sponsee say, "If my sponsor tells me to make a mud pie and eat it, I start digging."

I cannot say it better than that. Get a good sponsor—one who speaks your language—meet with them, work the steps aggressively, and do what they tell you to do. You'll be better off.

Einstein said the definition of insanity is doing the same thing over and over again, expecting a different outcome. Likewise, you can't stop doing the same thing over and over again and expect the same outcome. Don't stop going to meetings, meeting with your sponsor, and working the steps and expect to stay sober … that's crazy.

LEG FOUR: *Get the right pharmaceutical assistance*

George: *For years I was treated for depression. As it turns out, I was really suffering from anxiety that, when left untreated, manifested itself as depression. I was on one antidepressant for 14 years without ever being reassessed. Once I realized it was not working for me, I tried combinations and variations of drugs to address my disorders. Some work great for a short period of time and then their efficacy wanes. In other cases, the benefits are longer-lived. Regardless, medication is an important tool in my toolbox and I use it properly.*

What does using them properly mean?

Work with a psychiatrist to test various drugs to address your particular circumstance.

Be honest with them about what is going on in your life and how you are feeling. This is not an exercise in obtaining recreational drugs.

Seek advice and change the medications as and when needed.

Once the professional prescribes the drugs you need, take them—in the prescribed dosages and time frame.

Don't self-medicate or modify the schedule without professional advice.

As I mentioned before, if the prescription says, "Don't take this medication with alcohol," don't take the pills with water and then have a drink. It won't work. Trust me on that one.

SECTION III: THE DOING OF IT

Finding the Off Switch,
Writing the Mission Statement

Since addiction and the Monkey Brain are created by the hijacking within the emotional management system, then overhauling the management of one's emotional life is at the core of recovery.

Addicts operate on a creed: "I want what I want, when I want it!" Their emotional management system puts "want" in charge and follows wherever that leads. The conditioning process takes it from there, and over time—and repeated "want"-based thinking and behavior—an addict appears where a person used to be.

This new addict makes life decisions relying on the logic of "want"-created thinking errors. The Monkey Brain takes control to meet these wants and makes computations that lead to new paths of behavior, which are often perplexing and baffling to loved ones and friends.

Hidden from the consciousness of the addict, there develops a true fracturing of the self within. Even lifelong core beliefs and values cannot withstand the erosion of the sense of self brought on by addiction.

The Substance Abuse and Mental Health Services Administration (SAMHSA) has established a working definition that defines recovery as "a process of change through which individuals improve their health and wellness, live self-directed lives, and strive to reach their full potential."

It is that full potential we are seeking.

The Mission Statement

The beginning point is truly starting over. The mounting of a search to find our true self. The pre-addiction entity of our destiny, our best self, the one of potential met, not squandered. It is the goal of our personal recovery.

Characterizing that entity in words—describing the "who of what we are and want to become"—serves as the gateway to the path of recovering the self. These words become a document, a personal life mission statement that guides where we go from here.

Mission statements are the road map to the destination of recovery. They should be fairly short and include core values and beliefs, hopes and aspirations. A statement of who we want to be. Here is a sample:

In the past I have: abused drugs and acted out to avoid emotions and feelings of shame. My behaviors have led to the betrayal of my family.

But things are going to be different now. If not, the negative consequences are more than I can bear. I am changing who I am to be at peace with myself.

These qualities I want to gain: HONESTY! Patience, kindness and long-suffering, selflessness, gentleness, humility, meekness, patience, become full of love, and willing to accept life on life's terms.

Spiritually I want to discover; connect with my Higher Power.

With the rest of my life, I want to: stop letting addiction run my life and become the husband and father my family deserves.

The mission statement keeps us on track. It tells us whether we're building new pathways or using the old ones. It becomes a measuring rod for thoughts and actions to determine their appropriateness. It is the destination sought, and also the guide for each individual moment that creates a lifetime of existence. It replaces the old "I want what I want, when I want it" with a new standard of what it is that we desire. It is the new foundation of the emotional management system.

Read the mission statement often. Let it be a constant reminder of your goals. Let it help judge if thoughts and behaviors are taking you in the direction of the mission statement or if your Monkey Brain is exerting itself and using the same old addiction neural pathways.

New skills will allow us to live by the provisions of the mission statement. Recovery is the process of finding and building these skills. One of the first skills needed is awareness.

Skill Needed: Awareness

George's statement: "Admitting to myself that what I was doing wasn't working was the hardest thing I've done" is an admission of powerlessness, humility, and personal awareness. It is the very first of the recovery skills that lead to reclaiming the addicted brain and turning the Monkey Brain off.

The first half of awareness is the big picture, grasping of the true nature of one's situation, understanding what thoughts and behaviors have created. It is recognizing who we have become.

It begins with understanding our personality, behaviors, habits, emotional reactions, motivations, and thought processes. Having more self-knowledge not only helps make better choices but gives us understanding of our reactions to others. (Selfcreation.com)

Critical elements of self-awareness are core beliefs, strengths and weaknesses, passions, spirituality, relationship desires, likes and dislikes, feelings about money, and career choices.

While awareness of the big picture brings us to recovery, it is the moment-to-moment, second-by-second personal awareness that saves us from ourselves. Addicts, by definition, are not self-aware. Addicts are the opposite. They are self-absorbed, preoccupied with getting the next hit or high, solely concerned with preserving their ability to act out and live life on their terms.

Most live a double life, deluding themselves, pretending they are good citizens of the human family, while in reality they are lost in their addiction. A great deal of time and energy are spent defending and justifying both their ability and the opportunity to act out. Their second major battlefront is maintaining of appearances—the facade of normalcy. Awareness is the beginning of the end to all of that.

Without awareness, the mission statement will never be anything more than a statement. We will never find our way to where we want to be. Awareness is an imperative. Not "sorta" or "kinda" aware—or even aware some of the time—but the maintaining of conscious, meticulous awareness. Consistent, sustained awareness. That begins with honesty especially as it relates to ones "self."

AA teaches the use of "rigorous honesty," as an essential part of recovery work; it helps us identify the changes we need to make. Often, especially in the beginning, the insight of others who have walked the path help us to see what our Monkey Brain wants to deny. Listening to others who have successfully negotiated recovery is a Monkey Brain antidote. The fellow who writes his own recovery plan, will receive very little recovery from his plan. The Monkey Brain will see to that.

While exploring honesty and taking inventory, we recognize the successes along the way as well as the cringeworthy moments of life. The goal is to bring yourself to the on ramp of the "I can do better than this" road so that pondering a change of course can take place. That pondering will invite forward movement along the change continuum.

To bring awareness down to the current moment, ask the questions: What am I feeling? Why is this here? What is my part in this? What do I need? How would my "best self" play this out?

This monitor should never be turned off. Awareness is being in touch, constantly and continuously, with the forces in play. Ask these question regularly during the day.

One of the first difficulties we come across on the quest for awareness is the realization that addicts have little or no connection with inner feelings and emotions. This is the result of the one-size-fits-all remedy of acting out.

We begin to reconnect with our feelings by first gaining sobriety. We will not make much progress without it. Sobriety allows the clear view of our emotional self without the interference of our drug of choice. In some ways, it is like learning a new language. We have lost (or never had) the ability to translate the messages embedded in our feelings. With Monkey Brain working, when our feelings speak to us, we only hear a confusing gibberish that we recognize as the urge to use.

An addict doesn't need or want to be connected to feelings. As a matter of fact, addicts will do just about anything to avoid feelings. Feelings are difficult and complicated, and the solution for feelings is always the same: our drug of choice. By this logic, over time, addicts let go of connection to feelings and self since connection simply serves no purpose in their emotional management system.

Regaining contact with our feelings begins with regaining the ability to identify our emotions. Next, we must learn to decode the signals they are sending us. Then, within the context of our mission statement, we can observe and use the direction and guidance our feelings provide for our thinking and problem-solving.

It is also important that we gain an understanding of our emotions' underlying sources. These underlying issues may be areas that need our attention. If we carry the burden of childhood abuse, abandonment, PTSD events, and the like, their residual effects will get in the way of any healing. Their gravitational pull on our emotional management system pulls us off course. They must be resolved. That often requires therapeutic help from outside ourselves.

When we become proficient in the management of our emotions, we will be able to use their input as we make life choices. All emotions bring us information—those we enjoy feeling and those we dread all have their place in our processing. Processing those messages constructively becomes possible with awareness.

How To:

- Presented here are some exercises to improve your awareness. Try them all and see which ones work best for you. Take what you like and leave the rest.

- One cautionary word: if one of these really makes you feel uncomfortable, try it anyway. Thinking about why the activity makes you uncomfortable is an awareness exercise in itself.

- Work on big picture awareness by writing 100–500-word essays or creating bullet point lists for each of the following topics: my core beliefs, strengths and weaknesses, passions, spirituality, gratefulness, relationship desires, likes and dislikes, feelings about money, and career goals.

- Work on "in this particular moment" awareness by emotionally reconnecting with the simple practice of asking yourself several times a day: "What am I feeling? Why is this here? What is my part in this? What do I need? How would my 'best-self' play this out?"

- It always works best if you're working with your quiet self. Quiet the mind and emotions—no racing mind or raging emotions. If you're in the middle of an emotional storm, let it pass before doing your work. It will interfere with the process. (See Quieting Self.)

- Try to verbalize your feelings in your inner dialogue and by expressing what you feel to others that you trust. Expressing your feelings by writing also has a profound ability to advance awareness.

- Keep a recovery journal. We often find insights in writing that escape us otherwise. Things come out of our pen that will not come out of our mouths or inner chatter. Write regularly. Include any "aha" moments, quotes that inspire you, struggles, and recovery experiences.

- Review interactions with others by asking the following: "What did I feel? How emotional was I? Did I accurately express my feelings? What could I have done better?"

- Become acquainted with words that describe feeling. Connect them to what is going on inside of you.

Skill Needed: Accountability

When we accumulate enough awareness and add enough honesty, we can participate in the act of accountability. It is a benchmark of recovery. Accountability can only exist when the Monkey Brain is turned off and the addict takes ownership of their behavior.

Another reality is that we can be honest all day long, but if we fail to hold ourselves accountable to our honest truths, we have accomplished nothing. The Monkey Brain is still in control.

Accountability is defined using words like responsibility, answerability, ownership, and liability. Accountability acknowledges our successes and failures. In healing, it is saying that we messed up, we fell short, and are endeavoring to do better while repairing the damage as best we can. It is the taking of responsibility for our actions—for our treatment of others, and for the treatment of ourselves.

Accountability is the absence of playing the victim card, or the blaming of others for something we've done.

Accountability is honesty turned into action. Every day should include time for reflection and review of how the day went (from the context of recovery) and a healthy application of accountability administered. This is part of the "work" of recovery.

The harvest of accountability, when applied to the mission statement, is recovery.

The clinic of honesty and accountability is where thinking errors go to die. The insanity of these thinking errors is revealed for what they are: insane. They lose their power and dysfunctional comfort when the honest light of accountability illuminates them. Confession has almost a magical healing result, non-use of the addict voice can change everything, and finding a healthy non-victim stance puts us in the recovery position.

The headwaters of addiction are found in isolation, a location beyond accountability. We begin to leave our addiction when we can destroy the isolation and get out of our secret world. The Whitebook of Sexaholics Anonymous states: "The spiritual connection begins here. By first disconnecting from what we did. And we disconnect from it by sending it away from us as we tell it. This is the point of breakthrough. Or said more simply: Kill the secrets; kill the addiction."

George: *One of the catch phrases I use to keep myself honest in recovery is, "I am only as sick as my secrets." That helps me be truly honest in deciding if I'm hiding something for some reason. When I realize I am keeping a secret, an alarm bell goes off and I ask myself the hard questions of what am I feeling and why.*

The "addict voice" is the manifestation to the world of our Monkey Brain. These are the out-loud statements of our convoluted thinking. Addict voice is an art form. Blending truth and thinking errors in such a way that others accept our logic as sound.

George came to understand his addict voice this way: *I remember watching cartoons showing a kid trying to make a decision with the devil sitting on one shoulder and an angel sitting on the other shoulder, both telling him what to do. It usually involved something silly like taking an extra piece of cake, or another kid's toy—something with a moral dilemma.*

Now I knew that wasn't real, but I wished my addict voice was like that, sitting on my shoulder wearing the devil's suit and speaking in a high-pitched, squeaky voice, so I could easily identify and ignore him. What I came to realize was that my addict voice sounded just like the sane me: rational, calm, logical, and reasonable. The problem was that what he was telling me to do was crazy, usually with the same end in mind: trying to kill me."

Our addict voice doesn't have to be running very long before we end up in a "victim stance." Accountability and victim stance cannot coexist. Someone in victim stance has no responsibility for anything—it is always someone else's fault.

Dr. Paula Durlofsky notes, "The victim stance is a powerful one—the victim believes he or she is always morally right, is not responsible or accountable for their actions, and is entitled to sympathy from others."

Victim stance sounds like this:

"No one understands me."

"My boss is a jerk, so I don't need to listen to him."

"If my spouse would just understand and treat me better."

The core danger of victim stance is the belief that if you're the victim of something or someone, then the rules don't apply to you. Victim stance cashes in at the entitlement window. It is the ultimate "get out of jail free" card. Addicts can't stop using it, because if it isn't their fault, they don't have the responsibility to change anything.

Accountability goes both directions, forward and back. We not only need to be accountable for what we do today and going forward, we need to take responsibility for what is behind us. It is called the making of amends. Accountability for the past frees us from its grasp on us, the shame we carry because of it. It is a very important part of recovery.

Confession plays an integral part in that healing process. Confession can activate accountability. Making amends closes the deal. It's a benchmark of progress when an addict can articulate their acting-out behaviors (without minimization) in front of another human being. In reality, actual recovery cannot start without it, if it is missing, there is only the appearance of recovery.

The working of the 12 Steps, guide us to achieving accountability. The assignment: Work them! Beware: your Monkey Brain isn't going to like this assignment. It will generate a thousand reasons why you don't need to. Some of those reasons will be terribly compelling to you. These thinking errors are the last desperate act of a dying dysfunction. Ignore them.

Some struggle intellectually working the 12 Steps. There are many arguments: they are outdated or unnecessarily spiritually based. Objection noted. Approach it how you may, but recovery requires the accomplishment of the body of work involved in the steps in some therapeutic-like process.

George: *Another couple of my recovery gems:*

Religion is for the people who want to discuss hell; spirituality is for those who have been there.

For those who believe, no proof is required; for those who don't, no proof is sufficient.

If you're an anti-12 Stepper, please don't launch into your brilliant exposé of why the 12 Steps are not a good recovery process. That may be short-sighted and possibly a manifestation of your denial. It is denial by avoidance.

How To:

- Read your mission statement often to keep your goals in focus. Have check-ins with yourself about your progress.

- Bring structure and planning into your daily life. Plan to be accountable. Make your recovery your first priority.

- Find an accountability partner or buddy who knows your goals and plans—someone you can check in with regularly.

- Use your recovery group as a forum for your personal accountability.

- Do the work of Step 4. Make a searching and fearless moral inventory of yourself.

- Do the work of Step 8. Make a list of all persons you have harmed, and become willing to make amends to them all.

- Practice Step 10: Continue to take daily personal inventory (especially in regard to your mission statement), and when wrong, promptly admit it. (AA Twelve Steps)

Sponsoring

George: *In my experience, nothing helps me learn a subject like trying to teach it. When I finished working the steps, my sponsor said the first thing he wanted me to do was to take on sponsees. The idea of working with someone else in the program scared me to death. I only had a year of real sobriety myself and in no way felt qualified to guide someone else in such an important process. I wanted to withdraw, ponder what I had been through and spend some time licking my wounds. I just wanted to get on with my life and forget what I had been through.*

Despite my feelings, I did as I was told (remember, I am compliant child, people pleaser) and I picked up a few sponsees. Some didn't work out. Others did. The benefit of working with others became obvious very quickly. While I could not recognize crazy behavior when I was the perpetrator, I could easily identify it in others.

What that did for me was to help me be able to identify another's slippery behavior in myself and not fall back into the trap of my addiction. It also es-teemed me in ways I had not experienced before. Suddenly someone wanted to hear what I thought or felt and to learn from what I had done about my addic-tion. We would discuss very important issues and the sponsees identified with what I said and listened. This was a new thing for me, and I liked it.

Skill Needed: Acceptance

Acceptance is the next skill we seek. It can be practiced when we collect a subset of skills: "Turning it over," "Disputations," "Taking nothing person-ally," and giving up our "Need to control."

Acceptance: Skill One: Turning It Over

Worry is a good example to start with.

A Tolleism: "Worry pretends to be necessary, but serves no useful purpose." Let go of it. Much of the quieting of self is just that, letting go, sending it on its way, not giving harbor to the emotions that tend to overwhelm or the mind that can only race.

Letting go of things can be accomplished by turning it over. AA's third step reads: "Made a decision to turn our will and our lives over to the care of our Higher Power as we understood him." When we turn our lives and will over, we give up the need to wallow in negative emotions or let our mind race. We turn them over and do something else with our mind and emo-tional system (like truly experience the present moment.) Just let go of it.

It happened this way for one addict. *"The day I learned to turn it over was quite a day. Part of my acting out sexually was elaborate planning. Just thinking about how and when I was going to act out. I used to think it was just harmless fun until I realized it was part of my acting-out ritual. It was the beginning of the cycle for me. I really fixated on making my plans and wouldn't think about anything else. I couldn't turn it off. As I began my recovery and learned about turning it over, I decided that next time I* started one of my planning binges, I would turn it over. I was pretty excited to have a defense mechanism.

"At the time I had an hour-long drive to work. The down time of the drive had often been spent in one of my binges, and as I pulled out of my driveway, I started in. My mind knew the drill and went from 0 to 60 in no time. I thought I was ready with my new tool. I turned it over.

"If I think about this, I will act out, so I am going to turn this over and let it go.

"Immediately, I felt some relief and calming. I was very proud of my-self—for about 30 seconds; then I realized my planning binge was back. I turned it over. It came back.

"I turned it over. It came back.

"I turned on some very spiritual music. I turned my struggle over. It came back.

"I turned up the music and turned it over. It came back.

"I really turned up the music and turned it over. It came back.

"I started singing at the top of my lungs with the music and turned it over. It came back.

"And so my struggle ensued for nearly an hour. I was sweating, bawling, and nearly exhausted as I neared my destination, but I realized that the binge thinking had finally stopped. I guess my addict just wanted to know if I was serious."

Turning it over works for more than just troublesome thoughts. Emotions that challenge us can also be turned over. Anxiety, depression and other emotions can be turned over and left behind. Like this addict's experience, it may take some persistence and effort, but if we muster it, they will leave us. ("The Waterfall Concept: A blueprint for addiction recovery")

What do we turn over? Simple answer: anything beyond our ability to change or control our behavior in this exact moment. The right to road rage when we drive is an example. People are always going to be less than perfect drivers; some are intentionally reckless and threatening. But we are not the driving police. It is not our responsibility to rage at the absurdity of their ineptness or shout corrective judgments in their direction or even make digital signals for their consideration.

We cannot control how they drive. That is "on their side of the street," not ours. Let it go; take nothing from it. If we rage in self-righteousness, a chain reaction is set up in our Monkey Brain. Entitlement is created which is just this side of acting out.

Acceptance: Skill Two: Disputations

Another tool that is useful in quieting of self and the Monkey Brain is "Disputations." Disputations are the arguments our sober self can make when the Monkey Brain presents a thinking error.

Examples: When the Monkey Brain says, "No one will know," sober self can say, "But I will." When Monkey Brain says, "Just one won't hurt," sober self can laugh and say, "But it always has in the past; the first one leads to the second, to the third ..." Disputations are the implementation of accountability.

Disputations put into action the recovery skill of "playing out the tape." This skill, presented in many treatment programs, encourages the client to consider where following his urge might lead him. The idea is to consider or feel the consequences as a deterrent to acting out.

For example, an alcoholic might feel the urge to sneak a drink. His Monkey Brain is shouting things like, "I can handle this," or "You deserve it." His disputations might be: "I have never handled it in the past. What makes me think I will handle it this time?" Or simply, "What I deserve is to be sober."

For many addicts the most compelling disputations are created when considering what they might have said to their young pre-addict self. If we could go back in time, armed with current wisdom, fully aware of where this behavior will lead, what argument would we present in the face of the first use of our drug of choice. Those disputations often sound like this: "This doesn't seem like a big deal, right now, but it is going to lead to a lot of trouble and heartbreak for you down the road; walk away."

Addicts struggling with euphoric recall of their acting out successfully use this Disputation: "I shouldn't have done that then, and I sure shouldn't be doing it again in my mind now."

The final step when using Disputations is "turning it over." Dispute and let go.

How To:

- Make and memorize a list of Disputations for your known vulnerable moments (to work against your Monkey Brains favorite attacks).

- Samples:

- "No, I don't do that anymore."

- "I don't want to act out now. It's not on my plan for the day."

- "Doing that doesn't fit in with my mission statement."

- "That seems like a good idea right now, but it always turns out badly for me."

- "That's not within the bounds of my recovery."

- "I don't want to do it and have to confess to my spouse, home group, sponsor, etc."

- "I do not want to give up my sobriety—I have too much invested."

- "Yeah, I used to do that a lot, but not anymore!"

- "It is not the next right thing for me to do."

Acceptance: Skill Three: Don't Take It Personally

One of the major objectives of the Monkey Brain is to create entitlement. It is the "get out of jail free" card for addiction. The easiest access point of entitlement is the taking of things personally and creating a victim's stance. Justification and rationalization rise exponentially when we consider the wrongs that have been heaped upon us. Who can doubt our right when they consider the unfairness of our lives?

Don Miguel Ruiz in his Toltec wisdom classic, *The Four Agreements*, shares that the second agreement is based on the principle that we should not take anything personally.

He suggests three reasons:

- Nothing others do is because of you.
- What others say and do is a projection of their own reality, their dream.
- When you're immune to the opinions and actions of others, you won't be the victim of needless suffering.

"Needless suffering" we can do without. The fruit of the manufactured suffering is entitlement. From the position of entitlement, the addict can then send out purchase orders for the dysfunctional solution and remediation, which is endless acting out. Better to just let go—not take it personally, not create the needless suffering—than to hopelessly and endlessly try to find a comfort for our self-inflicted pain.

New clients, just beginning to travel the recovery highway, nearly universally need this wisdom. Many focus on their spouse, boss, or family. "If my wife would treat me differently"; "My boss is a jerk"; "My parents are a joke" are all statements that lead to needless suffering. Sex addicts struggle the most. "If my wife would just treat me better, I would be all right" comes out of their mouths in some form or another, created by experiences they have taken personally. "If only they loved me the way I want to be loved, my life would be so much better."

One addict practices acceptance by saying of his spouse: "That is Mary being Mary. I don't have to take it on or do anything about it."

It would be unusual, to say the least, if our life partner and friends were perfect. Since they are human and bound to do the falling short that humans do, our job is to practice acceptance and forgiveness. Forgiveness is something we need in bulk quantities for our own shortcomings. We can begin to accumulate it by giving it to others.

A great defense against taking things personally is to stay on your side of the street. Here's an example Edwin Crozier gave: "Last week we talked about keeping our side of the street clean. I know that sent some people over the edge. 'But Edwin, you just don't know my husband,' or

'But Edwin, you just don't know my wife.'

"Some folks went ballistic because they simply cannot see past their own victim mentality to ever notice their own wrong. 'Oh, sure, I mean I mess up sometimes. I'm only human. But my spouse (kid, parent, friend, neighbor, coworker, whatever) is so awful. Let me tell you the thousand ways my _____ is a jerk. How dare you suggest I should clean up my side of the street.'

"And thus, the vicious cycle continues until the relationship is absolutely destroyed. Your marriage ends in divorce. Your parents ostracize you. Your kids abandon you. Your friends avoid you. Your boss fires you. No doubt, you continue to live in the absolute certainty that all of this is everyone else's fault. It never occurs to you the only common denominator in your failed relationships is you." (Edwin Crozier)

To stay on our side of the street, we must let go of what others have done to us. That is their stuff—stuff we have no control over—and our mandate is to accept the things we cannot control.

How to Not Take It Personally

- Here is a collection of bullet points to consider in developing the ability to not take things personally:

- Be able to look at life with an "it is what it is" attitude.

- Accept that everything is not about you.

- Before reacting, create a space to consider things.

- Don't jump to conclusions; ask questions for clarity.

- Put yourself in others' shoes and consider things from their viewpoint.

- Don't dwell on it; no need to throw gas on the fire.

- What others do is beyond your ability to control.

- Develop greater empathy for others.

- Increase your own self-esteem.

- Let go of your perfectionism.

- Learn to accept criticism in a constructive way.

- Be okay with not being able to please everyone.

- Be on the lookout for level 10 responses to level 1 input — this is probably about YOU

Acceptance Skill Four: Giving up the Need to Control

Controlling behavior is defined as unduly trying to influence another's behaviors. A controlling person would criticize their partner's friends, clothes, body shape, thoughts, feelings, housekeeping, meals, level of sexual willingness—well, just about anything.

Controlling behavior is often parented by anxiety, and it is a symptom of our dis-ease with life. Therapeutic resolution of the underlying anxiety issues is indicated.

Controlling behavior usually comes out in a manipulative way that is abusive or borderline abusive, and it is very damaging to others and relationships. In terms of recovery, a controlling person is so consumed with managing others that they lack the ability to mount much recovery effort at all.

They get stuck because their "life management system" is to get others to act the way they want so they can live happily ever after. Managing everyone else leaves no energy for recovery. Besides, nothing is ever their fault. It's hard to fix yourself when nothing is your fault.

Controllers are fond of hissy fits and moodiness. They find anger a useful relationship management tool. Controllers often qualify as the poster child of passive-aggressive behaviors. Demeaning remarks, criticism, and shaming are tools of their trade. Controllers are often bullies; yet they are quite certain they are loving, giving people. Controllers are blind to themselves.

Controllers expect others to place personal priorities on the back burner and accept theirs. Probably the hallmark or signature behavior of a controlling person is the belief that if the spouse would just act differently, everything would be okay. If only the house were cleaner, if only you would lose a few pounds, if only you would take more interest in my hobbies, if only you would be more willing sexually … if only.

Controlling behavior is a merry-go-round the addict must get off of in order to approach recovery. It is not accessible from there. Controlling behavior denies the addict access to accountability, one of the major checkpoints on the passage to healing.

How to Be Less Controlling

Here are some points to consider when trying to overcome being controlling:

- Explore your relationship with anxiety and learn to better manage it.

- Develop a "no advice" policy.

- Accept that the best way to love someone is to let them be who they are—warts and all.

- Give up the need to be right all the time.

- Explore the idea of trusting and having faith in others.

- Consider if jealousy colors your thinking.

It's Serenity, Stupid

George: *My first introduction to serenity caused me to stop and think about what my life was like before (while I was actively acting out) and what it was like now. For the many years I acted out, I lived with an adrenalin rush. My acting out produced huge amounts of adrenalin, which I became addicted to. To stay high, I acted out, and when I stopped, the rush went away and I fell into withdrawal. Over time the need for adrenalin went away and I thought I was bored. What I was in reality was calm and—dare I say it—serene. That changed my paradigm of how I was feeling. It was no longer a bad thing; it was a good thing.*

Now Consider Acceptance

Much of quieting is accomplished by learning the art of acceptance. After all, the Big Book states that "acceptance is the answer to all my problems today!" Coming to understand how true that statement is in the addict's life opens the door to recovery.

Lori Destine shares, "Minor changes in thinking, I've found, lead to major changes in my reality."

One cannot live in a world (or reality) that they do not accept—even if it is the reality everyone else is living in. The purpose of Monkey Brain's creation was the establishment of a reality that allowed the dysfunction of addicted living. The foundation, rationalizations, and justifications of addiction grow out of the refusal to accept reality as it is.

Controlling behavior is a great example. Acceptance is the antidote to controlling behavior. As stated previously, the very strange thing about controlling behavior is that the only person who doesn't realize that he or she is being controlling is the very person trying to do the controlling. Another Monkey Brain masterpiece of blindness to reality.

Jan Zimmerman takes this view of not practicing acceptance: "When we decide the hows and whens of life, we are setting ourselves up for a disappointment. Life is bigger than us and vastly more complicated; and by trying to control it, we are not taking life on life's terms, but instead trying to impose our will on it, making life take us on our terms. We can see the evidence that we are doing this everywhere: "When we rage at traffic or the weather, when people disappoint us and we cannot forgive them, when we wish desperately to change things that are beyond our ability to change. Fighting against that which we cannot change is the surest way to meet with futility." (Jan Zimmermann)

The Serenity Prayer becomes our measuring stick for the invoking of acceptance. "God, Grant me the ability to accept the things I cannot change, courage to change the things I can and the wisdom to know the difference." Those things that are beyond our ability to change instantly become the items we must accept.

The skill of acceptance can never be achieved while we hold onto expectations. The widely quoted AA strategy is "Expectations are resentments waiting to happen. Resentment takes us in the opposite direction of acceptance. Hold none.

"Perhaps the best thing of all for me is to remember that my serenity is inversely proportional to my expectations. The higher my expectations of other people are, the lower is my serenity. I can watch my serenity level rise when I discard my expectations. But then, my 'rights' try to move in, they can too force my serenity level down. I have to discard my 'rights' as well as my expectations, by asking myself, 'How important is it, really? How important is it compared to my serenity, my emotional sobriety?' And when I place more value on my serenity and sobriety than anything else, I can maintain them at a higher level." (The Big Book)

If you can't accept life the way it is, you have a big problem because we cannot change what already has happened. Resisting the flow of life will only make you unhappy.

"The other choice is to bite the bullet and accept life the way it is. That takes courage, but the process will empower you enormously. The ability to let go of things in everyday life makes for happiness and ease. You can even laugh when you miss a bus that's departed five minutes early." (Axel Gjersten)

George: *Resentments have been defined as a poison pill you take, hoping the other person will die. By definition they are something you want to avoid at all costs because at best they are ineffective and at worst self-destroying.*

A word about your addict:

George: *We have seen the movie sequence many times: the good guy lies bleeding on the floor, shot and apparently mortally wounded. The antagonist walks over and stands above him gloating, when out of nowhere our hero brandishes a hidden weapon and shoots him dead. As the words "the end" appear across the screen, the audience applauds, assuming the hero will live happily ever after.*

In interpreting this movie scene in the context of addition, the addict is the good guy in the above scene—not that we like him and want him to survive. No. Instead, our addict is the one with a hidden weapon that he pulls out of nowhere and shoots you dead. Even if you're convinced you've killed him, he leaves one form and creates another, oftentimes more cunning, baffling, and powerful than before. The addict never dies. He merely goes into hiding, changes form, and waits for a good time to try again. I have heard it many times in meetings that while we are there, our addicts are in the parking lot doing push-ups. Ain't it the truth?

Skill Needed: The Quieting of Self

"I am an old man and have known a great many troubles, but most of them never happened." (Mark Twain)

Armed with our newfound awareness, honesty, and accountability, we can not only begin to turn off the Monkey Brain, but we also might even be able to unplug the darn thing. The next recovery action is to quiet self and come into the moment, or, said another way, become emotionally quiet and present. This clears the runway for the arrival of clarity.

Without quieting, the Monkey Brain engages in a succession of investigations of "bright shiny objects" that attract attention and occupy the mind. It is the meandering path the "I want" addict mind follows. It leads to an orgy of thinking errors. The quiet self is like a pond with no ripples and immune to bright shiny objects.

Addicts in recovery rooms, searching for healing, speak about "getting all up in the head." Recounting their last struggles, they begin, "I got all up in my head," just before recounting the failure of the week. "I got all up in my head … then my wife changed the locks … then I acted out … then a big fight ensued." Quieting is a treatment option for "getting all up in your head."

The aware self becomes the watcher or observer, preparing to assume the role of the operator of the mind and the tender to emotions. The quest is to find the true self that is described in the mission statement. Stepping out of "operator or watcher" mode leaves the mind unattended, free to wander from resentment to resentment, to lust, or race through the self's arguments of justification. Emotions follow, produced from what the mind is considering—anger, anxiety, desire, resentment, the whole lot of negative emotions may follow.

If enough gas is thrown on the fire, the emotions rage. These events obscure the true self. The racing of the mind and raging of emotions changes the landscape of our reality, creating a world not bound to truth and objectivity. It is the spawning ground for thinking errors and denial. It is the home of rationalization and justification. It is the base from which the addiction launches its attacks.

Some utilize the adrenaline rush of the racing mind or the power of raging emotions to medicate their pain. Raging emotions for some are an attempt at empowerment and emancipation. Anger and rage can make us feel like Samson for a minute, but our emotional building always collapses in the end. Some forestall the inevitable by staying endlessly angry.

Unfortunately our racing mind or raging emotions do not lead to freedom but only to a dysfunctional abyss that doesn't allow healthy relationships. They manufacture beliefs that are internalized. ("My wife is selfish"; "my kids show me no respect"; "my boss is always on my back.") Such inaccurate deductions create a world known only to the addict, separate from the reality family and friends are living in. The next stop for that train is entitlement—the notion that because of the suffering endured, acting out is deserved. Not a good stop for anyone seeking sobriety to get off.

Quieting of self is turning all that misinformation off. It is built on the AA wisdom of "accepting life on life's terms" and a principle of the Four Agreements, "take nothing personally."

Quieting of self is designed to stop any mind racing or the raging of emotions. As Tolle teaches, "The mind is the primary source of human suffering." True especially when a Monkey Brain is involved. Unplugging Monkey Brain and quieting of self eliminates the suffering at its source.

Self-talk or inner chatter plays a pivotal part. You talk to yourself constantly … and you become the architect and creator of the emotions you later experience through this self-talk.

"Emotions do not come as the result of an observation or an experience but rather as the result of the things we say to ourselves about those situations. Thus two people can have the same experience or observe the same event and come away with very different conclusions and emotions." (Sorensen, 1998)

George: *One tool I practice using all the time when I talk to myself is that the glass is neither half full nor half empty, it is just half a glass of water; there is no emotional energy in it.*

Cleaning up inner chatter and self-talk is a critical piece of recovery. The Monkey Brain uses inner chatter based on thinking errors to create the addict. Some try to use their Monkey Brain to find recovery. That never ends well. The Monkey Brain is always puking out bad decisions that keep the addict trapped. The Monkey Brain is in need of an overhaul, "reclaiming," if you will.

Monkey Brain's inner chatter comes with a judgmental feature, most often (and most harshly) turned on ourselves.

Everyone has a critical inner voice, but some have a more vicious and vocal inner critic. A loud, verbose inner critic is enormously poisonous to your psychological health, more than any deprivation or trauma you may have experienced. We can often heal our wounds and recover from our losses, but the critic is always with us, judging us, blaming us, finding fault in us.

"One of the most powerful ways to quiet our inner critic is through self-compassion. Compassion is the greatest antidote to the poison of your pathological inner critic. When you are being compassionate toward yourself, you essentially gag your pathological inner critic." (Beverly Engel MFCT)

Freedom from the pathological inner critic stops the life-draining hemorrhaging so that healing can begin. It takes us away from our favorite judgments, rationalizations, and victim thinking. It is not unlike the construction crew that clears the brush and debris from their site so there is a clean pad to work on.

George: *Early on in my recovery history, my therapist asked me, "Who do you converse with most during the day?"*

I said, "My coworkers, my wife, my boss, I guess."

She smiled and reminded me that I also spoke to myself all day long and that this constant conversation had a significant impact on how I viewed things and how I felt about life.

Then she asked, "What do you say when you make a mistake, like drop or spill something?"

"That's easy," I said, "What an idiot; you're such a klutz/jerk."

She went on to ask me about what my parents said to me as a child. Did they ever call me: stupid (Yes), bad (Yes), unworthy (Yes), ungrateful (Yes), spoiled (Yes), not as good as your brother (Yes). So these messages are recorded and are played back at the appropriate or inappropriate time. The toxicity of some of this internal dialogue is obvious.

One of my sponsees came back from a long weekend with his family in a very depressed mood, feeling sorry for himself and generally hopeless. He said, "My relatives spent the whole weekend pushing my buttons. I couldn't wait to leave."

I commented, "You know why they're so good at that? They know exactly how to push your buttons because they installed them all." My family is the same way. When I interact with them a single word or expression can bring up all sorts of negative self-images that were drummed into me when I was young. What you should learn from this is that in many cases, these messages are not true—and repeating them only deepens the rut of low self-esteem.

At one point my therapist asked me to describe what I was like when I was acting out in my sex addiction. Specifically what I was thinking and how did I treat people. This question elicited a ten-minute tsunami of self-hatred and self-loathing that overwhelmed her.

She then asked me if I would describe the other men in my program the same way.

"Of course not," I said. "They're generally really nice guys who have had some tough breaks and made some really bad decisions."

Then she asked, "Why are you so accepting of them and so hard on yourself?" All I could muster in response were tears. I could not answer that question.

In 1990, my very first therapist gave me a Post-it note with the words, "You are loveable and capable" on it. She asked me to keep it somewhere so I could see it every day. I put it on my dressing room mirror so I could see it as I tied my tie before going to work.

I saw it every day, and my reaction was generally the same: "Yeah, right. What does she know?" Not to be depressing, but it took me 20 years and a lot of recovery work before I finally believed it.

The importance of focusing on self-talk is that is the fodder of the addict. Your addict has a PhD in co-opting this communication, making you believe some of the craziest things. Your addict is definitely a devil character; however, he doesn't sound like a devil. He sounds just like you do in your sanest and most rational moment. So, his input gets mixed in with all your other self-talk. And when it is mixed with toxic messages from childhood, it can have disastrous results.

You can do really harmful things to yourself as a result. It helps to remember that your addict has only one objective: to kill you. So anything he says or does has that as its mission statement. When he sounds normal and is mixed in with all these other negative messages, it can be devastating—if not lethal.

How to Quiet Oneself

Here are some tools you can use to quiet yourself, to learn to be conscious and in the moment:

• Explore this particular moment. Situate yourself comfortably, empty your mind, and explore the elements of this particular moment. Focus on the input of your physical senses: what do you feel (physically), what do you smell, taste, hear, and see? For several minutes (or until quiet) slowly and deliberately verbalize what you notice: I see the desk, I smell the flowers, I hear the clock ticking …

- Exercise: Empty your mind, close your eyes. Breathe in slowly for a count of five seconds. Then exhale for five seconds. Focus your attention on the rising and falling of your chest or abdomen, the feel of the air coming in and going out. Focus on the backs of your eyelids; send any intruding thoughts away and do not follow them. Repeat until you feel calm and quiet.

- Explore in your memory activities that produce the most calm and peace. What are you doing when you feel emotionally quiet?

- Use guided imagery and affirmation recordings to supplement your ability to quiet yourself.

- Establish your emotional "safe place." Describe it in great detail and be able to experience it as if you were actually there. Utilize visiting there as needed.

Don't Stop Doing the Things that Work and Expect to Stay Sober

George: *If you've been in recovery for any length of time, you have heard the definition of insanity: "doing the same thing over and over again, expecting a different outcome." The reverse is also true. If you stop doing the same thing over and over again, you won't get the same outcome. You cannot stop going to meetings, meeting with your therapist, taking your meds, and working with your sponsor and expect to stay sober. That's crazy—in case you didn't know.*

Skill Needed: Living in this Particular Moment

"When people are not in the moment, they're not there to know that they're not there." (Ellen Langer)

This moment is all we really have. It is where we physically exist. Our emotional goings-on should have this same address. Living within this moment is best accomplished by assuming the role of watcher or observer.

When we spend our time in anxiety about future events or suffering yet again from our shame of the past, we are participating in our dysfunction. Emotional and mental dysfunction, anger, judgments, rationalizations, justifications, and the like create a residue, a bevy of dark, difficult feelings. It is the harvest that takes place when we experience a racing mind or let emotions rage. The residue is toxic. When we continue to add on by wallowing in our self-righteousness, entitlement emerges. It is a harvest best left in the field.

With accumulation and repeated harvests, the residue becomes formidable, taking on a life of its own. It may even become the driving force in our lives. Our dysfunction believes it to be the presentation of our needs, but the reality is simply that it represents the wants of our brokenness, masquerading as needs.

The residue can be made from many ingredients. Resentments, jealousy, frustration, lust, greed, anger, hatred, fear, insecurity—most any negative emotion will do. Freedom from the residue accumulating in our lives is found by practicing the skill of living in this particular moment, allowing our quiet self to practice our newfound skills of awareness, accountability, and acceptance.

This particular moment is it—all we have. Past moments are but unchangeable history now. The future, not yet conceived, is not real; we cannot successfully abide there. No amount of manipulation, worry, or future tripping will change anything about what lies ahead of us. Yes, to be prudent, some planning and preparing is necessary. But beyond that, worry and future tripping are futile. Here, now, in this moment, is where our life is.

It is important to realize that we are not our thoughts. Thoughts are just the manufacturings of our brain. A tool we have been supplied with. Our thoughts need to be processed through the filter of our awareness, rather than handing over life's control to them.

"Ordinary thoughts course through our mind like a deafening water-fall," writes Jon Kabat-Zinn. That water feature can carry our lives away unless we step out of the turbulence, "rest in stillness, stop doing and focus on just being." (Jay Dixit)

We come into the moment by first quieting ourselves, both mentally and emotionally, and stay there by observing, watching, and practicing our newfound skills.

How to Live in the Moment

"You can [live in any particular] moment just by paying attention to your immediate experience. You can do it right now. What's happening this instant? Think of yourself as an external witness, and just observe the moment. What do you see, hear, smell? It doesn't matter how it feels—pleasant or unpleasant, good or bad—you roll with it because it's what's present; you're not judging it. And if you notice your mind, bring yourself back. Just say to yourself, 'Now. Now. Now.'" (Jay Dixit)

Socialize with Other Sober People

George: Besides working with a sponsor or sponsee, it's important to surround yourself with people who speak your language and know where you've been. It will help provide a sounding board when you're in pain or doubt, or edgy. Addicts get addicts. Non-addicts think they do, but for the most part they don't. So it is good to have someone you can share your thoughts with who is not judgmental and shaming.

I know for me that no amount of therapy was going to help because the therapists did not speak my language. I am part of one group of men who get together for a weekly meeting as they want to include a more religious tone to their recovery. Although I'm not of their religion, they invited me to attend and I found the meeting to be very intimate and stimulating. I drop in whenever I can to stimulate my recovery in another way.

Skill Needed: Forgiveness, Including Emptying the Shame Closet

George: *A simple definition I use is: "Guilt means I did something bad. Shame means I am bad regardless of what I do."*

I've formulated my own simple definition of shame as follows: "The unwillingness or inability to accept our imperfections." The shameful person cannot tolerate his flaws and mistakes. Rather than tell himself, "I made an error," his inner critic screams, "I made an error and I'm worthless!"

While shame has its place in our emotional management system, an overdose is harmful. John Bradshaw terms it "toxic." Constantly berating ourselves wears us down and harms our relationships, spins us into anxiety and depression, prevents us from reaching goals and limits our success, and may even take a physical toll on our immune systems. (Seth C. Kadish) It also presents the opportunity for the medicating need for our addictive acting out.

A hallmark of shame is a constant awareness of our defects. Without realizing it, we become continual victims of shame-based thinking. Every day, we focus on our failures. Every day, we re-convince ourselves that we are defective. Our thoughts become riddled with judgment, regret, and images of impending failure. (Hazelden)

How to Deal with Shame

Here are some questions that are antidotes to shame:

• Is this thought really true?

• How do I know it's true?

• What is the evidence for this thought?

• What is the evidence against this thought?

• Can I think of any times when this thought has not been true?

- Is this thought helping me or hurting me?

- Who would I be if I let go of this thought?

- What could I do if I let go of this thought?

- Am I willing to release this thought?

- What's the worst that could happen if I let go of this thought? Can I live with that? (How to Change Your Thinking About Shame, Hazelden)

Sobriety Does Not Mean Recovery

George: *I never realized it, but for the first few years I was working the program, I was really a white knuckler. I was hanging on as tight as I could to stay sober, but recovery was a long way off. I believe this behavior is centered around Steps 1 through 3. The white knuckler has not come to terms with step 3 and keeps trying to hang on to some element of control they think they have. Yes, you can stay sober that way, but recovery will be elusive. Instead of leading a new life, you will be leading you old life under new rules.*

Sobriety Doesn't Mean Recovery ... STILL

The underlying philosophy of AA is that we stop drinking, straighten out our lives, and serve others. It is in the serving of others that we find recovery. Getting outside of ourselves far enough that we can do some good for others. We are not capable of that until we have some good sobriety.

Our addictions are grown in fields of dysfunction. The meadows of self-pity, entitlement, selfishness, arrogance, fear, anxiety, anger or perhaps the back forth of pain, loneliness, and brokenness. Once again we become the personification of "we want what we want, when we want it!" Cleaning up the character defects and ridding our growing fields of the behaviors that support the process of addiction take a lot of work after we find sobriety.

Remember our adopted definition of recovery: "A process of change through which individuals improve their health and wellness, live self-directed lives, and strive to reach their full potential."

On the recovery highway, recovery (full potential) is miles beyond sobriety.

The Monkey Brainer's "Must-Do List"

- Be brutally honest with yourself. If you lie to yourself, you cannot recover. This includes admitting that what you have become and have been doing isn't working, your life is unmanageable, and that doing the same thing over and over again and expecting different outcome is insane.

- Become willing to do whatever it takes to be sober. No half-measures or menu selections. If your sponsor says do something, just do it.

- Make a recovery plan. List the daily activities you plan on doing as part of your recovery work. Do them.

- Find a recovery fellowship that addresses your addiction and engage in it with full energy, attention, and participation. Attend meetings often, work a program, and find and work with a sponsor.

- Act sober until you can live sober, a.k.a. "fake it until you make it."

- Don't try to recover. RECOVER! Take a lesson from Yoda, "Try not. Do, or do not. There is no try."

- Do the next right thing.

- Don't do the next wrong thing. Recognize that your addict voice sounds as reasonable as your rational self. Understand that some of your self-talk is being created by an addict.

- Focus on what is real versus what you made up. Recall the "It's a beautiful mind." Are they really there?

- Peel the onion. Look to the reason you feel the way you do. Ask and answer the questions, "What am I feeling?" "Why am I feeling this?" "Is this real or am I making it up?"

- Feel your feelings, but don't let them rule your actions. If your reaction to a level 1 event is level 10, consider why you are so worked up.

- Seek zero tolerance to any acting-out thoughts or fantasies. (The three-second rule is a beginning point.)

- Be gentle with yourself. You didn't walk the first time you tried. Keep doing the right things until they become second nature.

- Do not take yourself too seriously. You're not the worst person in the world. To feel this way is a form of grandiosity. You're a good person with a serious problem. With proper treatment and actions, the problem can be left behind.

- Live in this particular moment. If you live in the past, you're in a state of regret. If you live in the future, you're in a state of anxiety. Only by living in the now can you make healthy decisions and recover.

If You Do This Over Time, You Will:

- Establish and maintain periods of sobriety.

- Achieve an emotional state of serenity, indicated by feelings of calmness, peace, reduced anxiety, and the absence of shame.

- Describe honestly and accurately to another human being your addictive behaviors and acting out without shame. This includes how you developed the addiction. Much of your recovery will be based on understanding how you got to where you are.

- Express accurately the feelings you're experiencing at any moment, to yourself and another human being.

- Let go of strong/knee jerk reactions; practice returning to serenity and living in this particular moment.

- Recognize and dispute your addict voice and the denial language you are using.

- Create and use your personal awareness to dismiss addictive thoughts and avoid addictive behaviors.

- Give up the need to control; accept the moment for what it is.

- Be open to inspiration; it often comes when you least expect it.

- Be a functional adult, dealing from strength and wisdom, making healthful decisions.

- Become your best self, improving your health and wellness, living self-directed lives, and striving to reach your full potential.

I Deserve to Be Sober

George: *As human beings I think we're trained to work for rewards. Study hard, get good grades, and you can go to a good college, i.e., the reward. Go to a good college, study hard, get good grades, get a good job, the next reward. Get a good job, work hard, get promotions and raises. Money, status, and a sense of accomplishment are the reward.*

When training pets, the same model is at work: reward good behavior and discipline bad behavior. Even in religion, we're told to lead our lives a certain way to get to heaven (the ultimate reward). Large parts of our existence are based on this work/reward model.

I'm sure something has happened in your life when you've said, "I've worked my butt off, I deserve _____ with the blank being things like: a hot bath, a cold drink, a glass of champagne, a good meal, a weekend at the beach, a night out with the boys/girls, etc." Most people make very functional work/reward decisions.

Then we have addicts. Addicts take this model and turn it on its ear. They use the work/reward system in a way that non-addicts find crazy. They build a reward system with several flaws in it.

First, the rewards they choose are not good for them. In reality they are actually a punishment and not a reward at all.

Second, the reward has a short shelf life—the "high" wears off quickly

Third, ever larger quantities of the reward are required to get the same feeling of euphoria.

Finally, too much of the reward kills. Be it alcohol, food, gambling, narcotics, sex, or whatever your "drug" of choice is, if you are an addict, your reward fits the above model.

For much of my life, which was spent mired in addiction, I kept score. I had several scoreboards, depending on what or who was bothering me at the time. Whenever something happened I didn't like, or whenever I was not loved the way I wanted to be loved, I never spoke up. I merely noted the infraction on my mental scoreboard and accrued points.

Larger infractions earned more points. Like every frequent flier knows, accrue enough points and you get a reward; for them, a free flight. For me, once I accumulated enough points, I would use this as justification to act out anew or to continue acting out, either with alcohol or sex. Those where my rewards for putting up with my life.

A huge stepping-stone for me was when I changed my paradigm to consider being sober in the moment, a caring and loving partner, and a benefit to society as my reward. No longer was I punishing myself but rewarding myself. I remember sharing at an AA meeting that I wanted to make the world a better place. And since the world is so huge, the only thing I can really do is not drink. And I know for sure the world is a better place when I don't drink.

The feeling of joy and serenity increased as I practiced this more. My fix became serenity. I can remember complaining to my sponsor that in recovery my life had become so boring—that nothing exciting was going on anymore. He merely stated, "You know what they call that; it's called serenity."